DATE DUE

JAN 24 1997

EATING HABITS
AND DISORDERS

GENERAL EDITORS

Dale C. Garell, M.D.

Medical Director, California Children Services, Department of Health
  Services, County of Los Angeles
Associate Dean for Curriculum
Clinical Professor, Department of Pediatrics & Family Medicine,
  University of Southern California School of Medicine
Former President, Society for Adolescent Medicine

Solomon H. Snyder, M.D.

Distinguished Service Professor of Neuroscience, Pharmacology, and
  Psychiatry, Johns Hopkins University School of Medicine
Former president, Society of Neuroscience
Albert Lasker Award in Medical Research, 1978

CONSULTING EDITORS

Robert W. Blum, M.D., Ph.D.

Associate Professor, School of Public Health and Department of
  Pediatrics
Director, Adolescent Health Program, University of Minnesota
  Consultant, World Health Organization

Charles E. Irwin, Jr., M.D.

Associate Professor of Pediatrics; Director, Division of Adolescent
  Medicine, University of California, San Francisco

Lloyd J. Kolbe, Ph.D.

Chief, Office of School Health & Special Projects, Center for Health
  Promotion & Education, Centers for Disease Control
President, American School Health Association

Jordan J. Popkin

Director, Division of Federal Employee Occupational Health, U.S. Public
  Health Service Region I

Joseph L. Rauh, M.D.

Professor of Pediatrics and Medicine, Adolescent Medicine, Children's
  Hospital Medical Center, Cincinnati
Former president, Society for Adolescent Medicine

THE ENCYCLOPEDIA OF
H E A L T H

PSYCHOLOGICAL DISORDERS
AND THEIR TREATMENT

Solomon H. Snyder, M.D. · General Editor

EATING HABITS
AND DISORDERS

Rachel Epstein

Introduction by C. Everett Koop, M.D., Sc.D.

Surgeon General, U.S. Public Health Service

CHELSEA HOUSE PUBLISHERS

New York · Philadelphia

The goal of the ENCYCLOPEDIA OF HEALTH *is to provide general information in the ever-changing areas of physiology, psychology, and related medical issues. The titles in this series are not intended to take the place of the professional advice of a physician or other health-care professional.*

Chelsea House Publishers
EDITOR-IN-CHIEF Nancy Toff
EXECUTIVE EDITOR Remmel T. Nunn
MANAGING EDITOR Karyn Gullen Browne
COPY CHIEF Juliann Barbato
PICTURE EDITOR Adrian G. Allen
MANUFACTURING MANAGER Gerald Levine

The Encyclopedia of Health
SENIOR EDITOR Paula Edelson

Staff for EATING HABITS AND DISORDERS
ASSISTANT EDITOR Laura Dolce
DEPUTY COPY CHIEF Nicole Bowen
EDITORIAL ASSISTANT Navorn Johnson
PICTURE RESEARCHER Georgeanne Backman
ASSISTANT ART DIRECTOR Loraine Machlin
SENIOR DESIGNER Marjorie Zaum
PRODUCTION MANAGER Joseph Romano
PRODUCTION COORDINATOR Marie Claire Cebrián

3 5 7 9 8 6 4 2

Library of Congress Cataloging-in-Publication Data

Epstein, Rachel S.
  Eating habits and disorders/Rachel Epstein; introduction by C. Everett Koop.
    p.   cm.—(The Encyclopedia of health. Psychological disorders and
their treatment)
  Includes bibliographical references.
  Summary: Describes the types of eating disorders and discusses their possible
causes, effects, and treatment.
  ISBN 0-7910-0048-6
      0-7910-0514-3 (pbk.)
  ·1. Eating disorders—Juvenile literature.
2. Nutrition—Juvenile literature. [1. Eating disorders.] I. Title.
II. Series.   89-22120
RC552.E18E67 1990   CIP
616.85'26—dc19   AC

CONTENTS

THE ENCYCLOPEDIA OF
HEALTH

THE HEALTHY BODY

The Circulatory System
Dental Health
The Digestive System
The Endocrine System
Exercise
Genetics & Heredity
The Human Body: An Overview
Hygiene
The Immune System
Memory & Learning
The Musculoskeletal System
The Neurological System
Nutrition
The Reproductive System
The Respiratory System
The Senses
Speech & Hearing
Sports Medicine
Vision
Vitamins & Minerals

THE LIFE CYCLE

Adolescence
Adulthood
Aging
Childhood
Death & Dying
The Family
Friendship & Love
Pregnancy & Birth

MEDICAL ISSUES

Careers in Health Care
Environmental Health
Folk Medicine
Health Care Delivery
Holistic Medicine
Medical Ethics
Medical Fakes & Frauds
Medical Technology
Medicine & the Law
Occupational Health
Public Health

PSYCHOLOGICAL DISORDERS AND THEIR TREATMENT

Anxiety & Phobias
Child Abuse
Compulsive Behavior
Delinquency & Criminal Behavior
Depression
Diagnosing & Treating Mental Illness
Eating Habits & Disorders
Learning Disabilities
Mental Retardation
Personality Disorders
Schizophrenia
Stress Management
Suicide

MEDICAL DISORDERS AND THEIR TREATMENT

AIDS
Allergies
Alzheimer's Disease
Arthritis
Birth Defects
Cancer
The Common Cold
Diabetes
First Aid & Emergency Medicine
Gynecological Disorders
Headaches
The Hospital
Kidney Disorders
Medical Diagnosis
The Mind-Body Connection
Mononucleosis and Other Infectious Diseases
Nuclear Medicine
Organ Transplants
Pain
Physical Handicaps
Poisons & Toxins
Prescription & OTC Drugs
Sexually Transmitted Diseases
Skin Disorders
Stroke & Heart Disease
Substance Abuse
Tropical Medicine

PREVENTION AND EDUCATION: THE KEYS TO GOOD HEALTH

C. Everett Koop, M.D., Sc.D.
Surgeon General,
U.S. Public Health Service

The issue of health education has received particular attention in recent years because of the presence of AIDS in the news. But our response to this particular tragedy points up a number of broader issues that doctors, public health officials, educators, and the public face. In particular, it points up the necessity for sound health education for citizens of all ages.

Over the past 25 years this country has been able to bring about dramatic declines in the death rates for heart disease, stroke, accidents, and, for people under the age of 45, cancer. Today, Americans generally eat better and take better care of themselves than ever before. Thus, with the help of modern science and technology, they have a better chance of surviving serious—even catastrophic—illnesses. That's the good news.

But, like every phonograph record, there's a flip side, and one with special significance for young adults. According to a report issued in 1979 by Dr. Julius Richmond, my predecessor as Surgeon General, Americans aged 15 to 24 had a higher death rate in 1979 than they did 20 years earlier. The causes: violent death and injury, alcohol and drug abuse, unwanted pregnancies, and sexually transmitted diseases. Adolescents are particularly vulnerable, because they are beginning to explore their own sexuality and perhaps to experiment with drugs. The need for educating young people is critical, and the price of neglect is high.

Yet even for the population as a whole, our health is still far from what it could be. Why? A 1974 Canadian government report attributed all death and disease to four broad elements: inadequacies in the health-care system, behavioral factors or unhealthy life-styles, environmental hazards, and human biological factors.

To be sure, there are diseases that are still beyond the control of even our advanced medical knowledge and techniques. And despite yearnings that are as old as the human race itself, there is no "fountain of youth" to ward off aging and death. Still, there is a solution to many of the problems that undermine sound health. In a word, that solution is prevention. Prevention, which includes health promotion and education, saves lives, improves the quality of life, and, in the long run, saves money.

In the United States, organized public health activities and preventive medicine have a long history. Important milestones include the improvement of sanitary procedures and the development of pasteurized milk in the late 19th century, and the introduction in the mid-20th century of effective vaccines against polio, measles, German measles, mumps, and other once-rampant diseases. Internationally, organized public health efforts began on a wide-scale basis with the International Sanitary Conference of 1851, to which 12 nations sent representatives. The World Health Organization, founded in 1948, continues these efforts under the aegis of the United Nations, with particular emphasis on combatting communicable diseases and the training of health-care workers.

But despite these accomplishments, much remains to be done in the field of prevention. For too long, we have had a medical care system that is science- and technology-based, focused, essentially, on illness and mortality. It is now patently obvious that both the social and the economic costs of such a system are becoming insupportable.

Implementing prevention—and its corollaries, health education and promotion—is the job of several groups of people:

First, the medical and scientific professions need to continue basic scientific research, and here we are making considerable progress. But increased concern with prevention will also have a decided impact on how primary-care doctors practice medicine. With a shift to health-based rather than morbidity-based medicine, the role of the "new physician" will include a healthy dose of patient education.

Second, practitioners of the social and behavioral sciences—psychologists, economists, city planners—along with lawyers, business leaders, and government officials—must solve the practical and ethical dilemmas confronting us: poverty, crime, civil rights, literacy, education, employment, housing, sanitation, environmental protection, health care delivery systems, and so forth. All of these issues affect public health.

Third is the public at large. We'll consider that very important group in a moment.

Fourth, and the linchpin in this effort, is the public health profession—doctors, epidemiologists, teachers—who must harness the professional expertise of the first two groups and the common sense and cooperation of the third, the public. They must define the problems statistically and qualitatively and then help us set priorities for finding the solutions.

To a very large extent, improving those statistics is the responsibility of every individual. So let's consider more specifically what the role of the individual should be and why health education is so important to that role. First, and most obviously, individuals can protect themselves from illness and injury and thus minimize their need for professional medical care. They can eat a nutritious diet, get adequate exercise, avoid tobacco, alcohol, and drugs, and take prudent steps to avoid accidents. The proverbial "apple a day keeps the doctor away" is not so far from the truth, after all.

Second, individuals should actively participate in their own medical care. They should schedule regular medical and dental checkups. Should they develop an illness or injury, they should know when to treat themselves and when to seek professional help. To gain the maximum benefit from any medical treatment that they do require, individuals must become partners in that treatment. For instance, they should understand the effects and side effects of medications. I counsel young physicians that there is no such thing as too much information when talking with patients. But the corollary is the patient must know enough about the nuts and bolts of the healing process to understand what the doctor is telling him. That is at least partially the patient's responsibility.

Education is equally necessary for us to understand the ethical and public policy issues in health care today. Sometimes individuals will encounter these issues in making decisions about their own treatment or that of family members. Other citizens may encounter them as jurors in medical malpractice cases. But we all become involved, indirectly, when we elect our public officials, from school board members to the president. Should surrogate parenting be legal? To what extent is drug testing desirable, legal, or necessary? Should there be public funding for family planning, hospitals, various types of medical research, and medical care for the indigent? How should we allocate scant technological resources, such as kidney dialysis and organ transplants? What is the proper role of government in protecting the rights of patients?

What are the broad goals of public health in the United States today? In 1980, the Public Health Service issued a report aptly entitled *Promoting Health-Preventing Disease: Objectives for the Nation.* This report expressed its goals in terms of mortality and in terms of intermediate goals in education and health improvement. It identified 15 major concerns: controlling high blood pressure; improving family planning; improving pregnancy care and infant health; increasing the rate of immunization; controlling sexually transmitted diseases; controlling the presence of toxic agents and radiation in the environment; improving occupational safety and health; preventing accidents; promoting water fluoridation and dental health; controlling infectious diseases; decreasing smoking; decreasing alcohol and drug abuse; improving nutrition; promoting physical fitness and exercise; and controlling stress and violent behavior.

For healthy adolescents and young adults (ages 15 to 24), the specific goal was a 20% reduction in deaths, with a special focus on motor vehicle injuries and alcohol and drug abuse. For adults (ages 25 to 64), the aim was 25% fewer deaths, with a concentration on heart attacks, strokes, and cancers.

Smoking is perhaps the best example of how individual behavior can have a direct impact on health. Today cigarette smoking is recognized as the most important single preventable cause of death in our society. It is responsible for more cancers and more cancer deaths than any other known agent; is a prime risk factor for heart and blood vessel disease, chronic bronchitis, and emphysema; and is a frequent cause of complications in pregnancies and of babies born prematurely, underweight, or with potentially fatal respiratory and cardiovascular problems.

Since the release of the Surgeon General's first report on smoking in 1964, the proportion of adult smokers has declined substantially, from 43% in 1965 to 30.5% in 1985. Since 1965, 37 million people have quit smoking. Although there is still much work to be done if we are to become a "smoke-free society," it is heartening to note that public health and public education efforts—such as warnings on cigarette packages and bans on broadcast advertising—have already had significant effects.

In 1835, Alexis de Tocqueville, a French visitor to America, wrote, "In America the passion for physical well-being is general." Today, as then, health and fitness are front-page items. But with the greater scientific and technological resources now available to us, we are in a far stronger position to make good health care available to everyone. And with the greater technological threats to us as we approach the 21st century, the need to do so is more urgent than ever before. Comprehensive information about basic biology, preventive medicine, medical and surgical treatments, and related ethical and public policy issues can help you arm yourself with the knowledge you need to be healthy throughout your life.

FOREWORD

Solomon H. Snyder, M.D.

Mental disorders represent the number one health problem for the United States and probably for the entire human population. Some studies estimate that approximately one-third of all Americans suffer from some sort of emotional disturbance. Depression of varying severity will affect as many as 20 percent of all of us at one time or another in our lives. Severe anxiety is even more common.

Adolescence is a time of particular susceptibility to emotional problems. Teenagers are undergoing significant changes in their brain as well as their physical structure. The hormones that alter the organs of reproduction during puberty also influence the way we think and feel. At a purely psychological level, adolescents must cope with major upheavals in their lives. After years of not noticing the opposite sex, they find themselves romantically attracted but must painfully learn the skills of social interchange both for superficial, flirtatious relationships and for genuine intimacy. Teenagers must develop new ways of relating to their parents. Adolescents strive for independence. Yet, our society is structured in such a way that teenagers must remain dependent on their parents for many more years. During adolescence, young men and women examine their own intellectual bents and begin to plan the type of higher education and vocation they believe they will find most fulfilling.

Because of all these challenges, teenagers are more emotionally volatile than adults. Passages from extreme exuberance to dejection are common. The emotional distress of completely normal adolescence can be so severe that the same disability in an adult would be labeled as major mental illness. Although most teenagers somehow muddle through and emerge unscathed, a number of problems are more frequent among adolescents than among adults. Many psychological aberrations reflect severe disturbances, although these are sometimes not regarded as "psychiatric." Eating disorders, to which young adults are especially vulnerable, are an example. An extremely large number of teenagers diet to great excess even though they are not overweight. Many of them suffer from a specific disturbance referred to as anorexia nervosa, a form of self-starvation that is just as real a disorder as diabetes. The same is true for those who eat compulsively and then sometimes force themselves to vomit. They may be afflicted with bulimia.

Depression is also surprisingly frequent among adolescents, although its symptoms may be less obvious in young people than they are in adults. And, because suicide occurs most frequently in those suffering from depression, we must be on the lookout for subtle hints of despondency in those close to us. This is especially urgent because teenage suicide is a rapidly worsening national problem.

The volumes on Psychological Disorders and Their Treatment in the ENCYCLOPEDIA OF HEALTH cover the major areas of mental illness, from mild to severe. They also emphasize the means available for getting help. *Anxiety and Phobias, Depression,* and *Schizophrenia* deal specifically with these forms of mental disturbance. *Child Abuse* and *Delinquency and Criminal Behavior* explore abnormalities of behavior that may stem from environmental and social influences as much as from biological or psychological illness. *Personality Disorders* and *Compulsive Behavior* explain how people develop disturbances of their overall personality. *Learning Disabilities* investigates disturbances of the mind that may reflect neurological derangements as much as psychological abnormalities. *Mental Retardation* explains the various causes of this many-sided handicap, including the genetic component, complications during pregnancy, and traumas during birth. *Suicide* discusses the epidemiology of this tragic phenomenon and outlines the assistance available to those who are at risk. *Stress Management* locates the sources of stress in contemporary society and considers formal strategies for coping with it. Finally, *Diagnosing and Treating Mental Illness* explains to the reader how professionals sift through various signs and symptoms to define the exact nature of the various mental disorders and fully describes the most effective means of alleviating them.

Fortunately, when it comes to psychological disorders, knowing the facts is a giant step toward solving the problems.

Food is crucial to life. It provides nourishment, is essential to growth, and can act as either a stimulant or a calming agent. Food also plays a role in both personal and professional activities; it can provide a backdrop for both romance and for business. Specific meals help to define holidays—what would Thanksgiving be without turkey, or the Fourth of July without a family barbecue? Indeed, a large part of people's social life revolves around food. For example, friends traditionally meet over dinner or lunch. In addition, food plays a symbolic role in religious rituals. Christians eat wafers and drink wine during church services to re-create the sacrifice of Christ; Jews eat matzo (unleavened bread) during Passover to remember their ancestors' heroic journey from Egypt to Israel; and Muslims refrain from eating before sundown during the month of Ramadan to commemorate the first revelation of their holy book, the Koran.

Today, most people also want food to be convenient. There are fast-food restaurants, take-out pizza parlors, and delicatessens with 24-hour delivery. The microwave oven enables families to have a complete meal in just minutes, and the salad bar allows people on the go to select from a wide array of foods in record time.

Food is also used to reward or to punish: Good children are rewarded with a cookie; a new job or promotion will be celebrated with a dinner out. On the other hand, a child who has behaved badly may be sent to bed with no dinner. Parents tell their children that if they do not eat their vegetables, there will be no dessert.

But aside from all of its other roles, food is tied closest to personal appearance. Those who choose cottage cheese instead of cheesecake, and apples instead of apple pie, expect to be thin, and in modern society looking thin means looking good. Gelatin, it is said, helps nails grow. Drinking water clears the complexion; chocolate, some say, does the opposite.

All this talk of the importance of food is certainly not groundbreaking news. Even for those who had not thought before of the tremendous role food plays in society, reading about it may light a spark of recognition. Seen from another perspective, however, it might seem incredible that this much emphasis is placed upon food.

Sadly, though, some people do place an excessive and even dangerous significance upon eating, or not eating, food. Those who do so have what is known as an eating disorder. An eating disorder can be defined simply as an obsession with eating in the midst of an abundance of food. (Eating disorders rarely occur in countries where there is a scarcity of food supplies or among people who must worry where their next meal is coming from.)

Eating disorders fall into several distinct clinical categories. Perhaps the best-known eating disorder is *anorexia*. People suf-

A 17th-century engraving of the preparation of matzo for the Jewish Passover. Food such as matzo (unleavened bread) is an important part of many religious rituals and practices.

fering from anorexia starve themselves literally to the point of emaciation, even death. *Bulimia*, much like anorexia, involves periods of starvation interspersed with episodes of binging. During these episodes the sufferer gorges him- or herself with an extraordinary amount of food—very often junk food. After the binge, the bulimic purges—forcing him- or herself to vomit or using a large amount of laxatives or diuretics (drugs that rid the body of, respectively, solid and liquid waste). Another type of eating disorder, compulsive overeating, is a disease that involves frequent binging on enormous amounts of food. But why do people develop these disorders in the midst of plenty?

Assuming an adequate food supply, people develop eating problems when the emotional and appearance-related aspects of eating overwhelm their awareness of food's value as nutrition. The goal of this book, then, is twofold: First, it will give readers an idea of how to eat in order to maximize health, emphasizing the importance of basic nutrition that comes from eating healthy, well-balanced meals; second, it will explain how social, psychological, and biological factors can bring about eating disorders. With a full understanding of the symptoms and danger signals of eating disorders—and indeed of the seriousness of these diseases—readers may not only be less likely to develop an eating disorder but also more able to help if someone close to them develops such a disease.

•   •   •   •

CHAPTER 1

· · · · · · · · · · · · · · · ·

GOOD EATING HABITS: NUTRITION

It is obvious that not all of the food a person consumes over a lifetime remains in the body—indeed, all but a very small percentage of it is excreted. Yet food does help people grow from their newborn weight of 6 or 8 pounds to their adult weight, which may be as little as 15 or as much as 30 or more times that original weight. Even then, many people struggle to maintain their weight, which may far exceed what it should be or what they would like it to be.

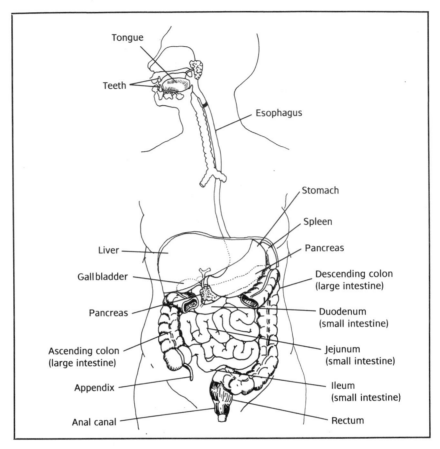

Tongue

Teeth

Esophagus

Stomach

Spleen

Liver

Pancreas

Gallbladder

Descending colon
(large intestine)

Pancreas

Duodenum
(small intestine)

Ascending colon
(large intestine)

Jejunum
(small intestine)

Appendix

Ileum
(small intestine)

Anal canal

Rectum

The organs of the digestive system are responsible for breaking food down to its most basic elements. These elements are then carried by the blood to the various cells of the body, where they are used as energy.

How is food processed by the human body? What parts stay in the body, and why? The answers to these questions lie in the digestive system—the body system responsible for processing food. The organs that make up the digestive system include the esophagus, the stomach, and the small and large intestines (together these organs constitute the *alimentary canal*—a 27-foot-long tube that begins at the mouth and ends with the large intestine), as well as two vital organs, the liver and the pancreas.

An efficient digestive system keeps the body healthy and strong and allows it to use food to its best effect. If the body does not receive adequate supplies of food, however, the digestive system will begin to digest body tissues in an effort to save the body's *cells* (the basic building blocks, or units, of the body) from dying. Under normal circumstances, it takes the digestive system 15 to 48 hours to digest a meal completely. Although food enters the mouth in small pieces, by the time it has gone through the digestive system it resembles a soupy paste. It is from this paste that nutrients—the parts of food that keep the body going—are extracted.

The human body needs three basic types of nutrients: *proteins*, *carbohydrates*, and *fats*. In addition, it requires a certain amount of *vitamins* and *minerals*. Naturally, all of these nutrients come from food. Proteins are found in meats, fish, egg whites, whole grains, and beans. They are vital to the body's functioning because they are needed by every cell for growth and repair. Proteins are also an emergency source of energy for the body.

The body has no way of storing proteins, however, so some must be ingested every day to ensure proper health. According to Jane Brody, nutrition columnist for the *New York Times*, "Even after just one day without protein, your body will begin to break down the protein in nonessential tissues, like muscles, and use it to reconstruct the proteins needed by organs vital for survival."

Carbohydrates, a second type of nutrient, are composed of carbon, hydrogen, and oxygen. They can range from simple sug-

The healthiest diet contains foods from the five basic food groups: dairy products, fruits and vegetables, grains, meat, and fish and poultry.

ars, which contain only a few carbon atoms, to complex compounds—such as starches—that are made up of large chains of simple sugars joined together to form a single unit. Simple carbohydrates, or sugars, can be found naturally in milk, fruits, vegetables, and nuts. Of course, they are also found in cakes, cookies, and pies. Although all simple sugars are identified by the suffix -ose (as in *fructose, sucrose, maltose*), they are all ultimately broken down in the body into glucose, a very basic molecule.

Starches, or complex carbohydrates, are found in breads, cereals, potatoes, rice, and pasta. Starches are also broken down into glucose. Carbohydrates are used as an energy source just like the other nutrients—in fact, most energy used in the course of the day comes from carbohydrates. This energy comes from the supply of glucose the body has stored for this particular purpose. If the body does not have a supply of glucose, it must burn fats, which can leave the body with an excess of *ketones*—fat waste products. Consequently, the person has less energy, and his or her organs and immune system may not be operating at peak efficiency.

Fats, a third type of nutrient, are found in milk products, egg yolks, nuts, meats, and oils. Although they are necessary for proper body functioning, according to Jane Brody a healthy person needs only one tablespoon of fat a day. The average American consumes many times that amount.

There is more than one type of fat. Saturated fats are found in meats and animal products such as butter. These fats are not needed by the body, and they contain *cholesterol*, a substance that, in excess, can cause serious damage (such as clogged arteries, a cause of heart disease) in the body. Polyunsaturated fats are found in vegetable oils such as corn oil, and in fish. The difference between saturated and polyunsaturated fats is purely chemical. If the carbon atoms that make up a fat molecule are surrounded by hydrogen atoms, the fat is said to be saturated. Polyunsaturated fats, on the other hand, contain fewer hydrogen atoms and do not cause cholesterol problems. Nonetheless, the body requires only a small amount of these fats.

Vitamins are organic materials supplied by plant or animal products. A certain amount of vitamins is essential for a healthy body. They help process carbohydrates, proteins, fats, and min-

ENERGY NEEDS THROUGH LIFE		
Ages	*Daily caloric need*	*Range*
Infants		
To 6 months	Weight in pounds × 53	43–66
6 months–1 year	Weight in pounds × 48	36–61
Children		
1–3 years	1,300	900–1,800
4–6	1,700	1,300–2,300
7–10	2,400	1,650–3,300
Males		
11–14	2,700	2,000–3,700
15–18	2,800	2,100–3,900
19–22	2,900	2,500–3,300
23–50	2,700	2,300–3,100
51–75	2,400	2,000–2,800
Over 75	2,050	1,650–2,450
Females		
11–14	2,200	1,500–3,000
15–18	2,100	1,200–3,000
19–22	2,100	1,700–2,500
23–50	2,000	1,600–2,400
51–75	1,800	1,400–2,200
Over 75	1,600	1,200–2,000
Pregnant	+300	
Nursing	+500	

*These daily caloric intakes are recommended by the Food and Nutrition Board of the National Academy of Sciences–National Research Council to meet the energy needs of average healthy persons. However, precise requirements may vary over a wide range, depending on height, weight, and level of activity.

erals and aid in the formation of blood, hormones, and nervous system chemicals.

Minerals originate in the soil and are extracted by plants and plant-eating animals. When humans consume these plants and animals in the form of vegetables and meats, they are ingesting these minerals. The body uses minerals for a variety of functions, including keeping the heart beating regularly. These minerals include *calcium* (a mineral that combines with phosphorus to form healthy teeth and bones and is essential to a regular heartbeat), *magnesium* (a mineral that makes up a part of cellular fluids and is utilized in the production of *enzymes*—substances produced by the body that regulate chemical reactions), and *sodium* (a mineral that enables the body to retain fluids and maintain blood pressure). The major cause of death in victims of anorexia is an inadequate supply of these minerals to the heart.

Because all these types of nutrients are required to keep the body healthy, a balanced diet would naturally include portions of foods from the five food groups: dairy products, fruits and vegetables, grains, meat, and fish and poultry.

All foods that are consumed are either used by the body for energy, given off as waste products, or turned into fat. Most dieters—and an astonishing number of people are on diets right now—are trying to prevent their body from turning food into fat. These dieters eat less and exercise more until their body is at their desired weight. Unfortunately, for many dieters this goal may seem unattainable, and in many ways it may be.

Scientists now believe that a person's body is "programmed" to weigh a certain amount and any attempt to lose weight beyond that amount will not be easily accepted by the body. Weight gained is expressed in *calories* (the common term for kilocalories)—a unit of heat needed to raise 1 kilogram of water 1 degree centigrade at 1 degree of atmospheric pressure—with 3,600 calories of food intake translating into 1 pound of weight. The rate at which the body burns up, or converts, calories to energy is known as the Basal Metabolism Rate (BMR)—or *metabolism*.

Although the term is often used to describe a person—"Sue is so thin, she must have a fast metabolism" or "Paul is so heavy, he must have a slow metabolism"—the rate of metabolism is not invariable. For example, metabolism usually changes over the

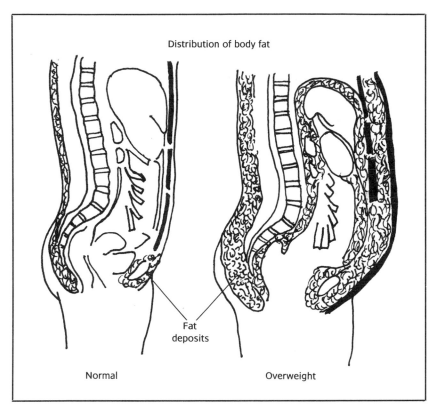

Distribution of body fat

Fat
deposits

Normal

Overweight

The excess fat in an overweight person (right) distorts the body and crowds internal organs.

course of a person's lifetime—becoming faster, or burning calories more quickly, when the person is young and slowing down when the person is older. Metabolism can also be voluntarily changed. Exercise, for example, speeds up metabolism, allowing the body to burn calories faster. Depriving oneself of food—starving oneself—will slow down one's metabolism.

In an ideal world, all calories would be used as energy. Unfortunately, this is not always the case. Excess calories are stored in fat cells, which make up *adipose tissue.* These fat cells, once created, remain permanently within the body. If a person's body requires more fat than it receives through food, it takes the fat it needs from the adipose tissue. The fat cells continue to exist but become smaller.

Until recent years, the logical explanation for weight gain and weight loss was that if a person took in more calories than he or she burned off, he or she would gain weight. If, on the other hand, that person burned off more calories than he or she took in, he or she would lose weight.

In the 1970s, researchers developed a different theory on weight gain and loss. This theory is known as the "setpoint theory." Dr. William I. Bennett, editor of the *Harvard Medical School Letter* and one of the physicians who strongly supports the setpoint theory, explains it this way: Adipose tissue, or tissue where fat is stored, is regulated within the body by an internal mechanism that measures the amount of stored adipose tissue. This internal mechanism then compares this figure with its own internal standard and minimizes the difference between the two.

Evidence that such a setpoint exists was uncovered by several studies. In 1950, while studying the effects of starvation on the body, Ancel Keyes, a professor at the University of Minnesota, discovered that men who lost 20% to 25% of their body weight found it increasingly difficult to lose the weight once they had progressed beyond the first few pounds. In discussing similar findings in studies on weight-loss programs, David M. Garner and his colleagues at the University of Toronto pointed out in the *Handbook of Psychotherapy for Anorexia Nervosa and Bulimia* that most obese people who had lost weight put it back on. In fact, only 5% of those who lost more than 20 pounds kept it off for 2 years or more. Conversely, in a 1968 study, Professor Ethan Allen Hitchcock Sims and his colleagues asked a group of prison volunteers to agree to gain 20% to 25% of their body weight. Although the men consumed twice their usual amount of calories, after putting on the first few pounds it became increasingly difficult for them to gain any more weight.

From these studies scientists were able to hypothesize that the human body sets its own weight goal and cannot vary from that weight without a struggle. The stability that comes with a setpoint, however, can be altered. Stress, advanced age, and a diet high in fats and sugars can all trigger the body to allow excess fat accumulation. On the other hand, exercise and smoking lower the setpoint, causing the body to tolerate less fat.

These studies offer an explanation of the problems of obesity and perhaps make it easier to understand why an obese person

Obesity

Obesity is, quite simply, a condition characterized by excess body fat. This does not mean, however, that a person five pounds overweight is "obese." Some physicians clarify obesity as being at least 20% over the recommended weight for a given height. According to this definition, a woman who is 5 feet tall and weighs 150 pounds is 25 pounds overweight—and obese.

The physical condition of obesity, which often begins in childhood, is often accompanied by psychosocial difficulties. Obese children are often treated poorly by other children, feel insecure about their looks, and may be unable to participate in sports activities.

As an adult, however, the complications of obesity are often life threatening. According to *The New Complete Medical and Health Encyclopedia*, the death rate for obese people between the ages of 20 and 64 is 50% higher than that for people whose weight is normal. This difference results from the increased risk of diabetes, heart disease, arthritis, high blood pressure, vascular disease, kidney trouble, and a number of other ailments to which obese persons are often subject. Obesity can also complicate surgical procedures. An overweight person requires larger amounts of anesthesia. Fat may make getting to the organ or surgical area more difficult. In addition, obesity can cause problems during pregnancy. Diabetes, edema, and high blood pressure may put a pregnant mother—and her child—at risk by complicating the labor.

Scientists have discovered that obesity is difficult to cure because it is a product of unhealthy eating patterns that have often been in place since infancy. In fact, the only sure cure for obesity is prevention—teaching good eating habits to children. A healthy diet early in life can spare a child a lifetime of obesity and its attendant complications.

would claim constant hunger. Researcher R. E. Nisbett of the University of Michigan has theorized that obese people may actually be in a constant state of hunger from calorie deprivation—that is, an obese person's setpoint requires a high number of calories to maintain itself. Dieting for these people is an endless battle against hunger pains and against an internal, physiologically determined setpoint. Although, according to most standards, these people are "statistically overweight," Nisbett points out, they are "biologically underweight."

With all of this talk about setpoint, it is easy to become discouraged about losing weight, or even about eating healthily. People should keep in mind, however, that diet combined with exercise can alter the setpoint and has allowed many overweight people to lose excess weight. The best precaution, however, against becoming obese and achieving a high setpoint is to learn how to eat properly as a child or, if not then, as a young adult.

The Guideline Approach to Good Eating

According to Dr. Michael Jacobson, the director of the Center for Science in the Public Interest in Washington, D.C., most Americans are not only well nourished but also overnourished. Jacobson believes that guidelines on what to avoid as well as what to eat may be a more efficient road to good health than the standard directive that claims one should eat from the five food groups (breads and grains, dairy products, meats, fruits and vegetables, poultry and fish) in order to maintain good health. In *The Complete Eater's Digest and Nutrition Scoreboard*, Jacobson explains that "the ravages of food excess . . . are by far the greatest nutritional problem in the U.S., Canada, and most other technologically advanced nations." This "excess" consists of too many calories and too much fat, salt, cholesterol, and alcohol.

Many studies, including the well-known Framingham, Massachusetts, nutritional study, have shown causal relationships between fat (particularly cholesterol) consumption and heart disease and between salt (sodium) consumption and high blood pressure, which is one of the conditions leading to heart attacks. A study conducted by the eminent British surgeon Denis P. Burkeitt also indicated that following low-fiber and low-carbohydrate diets may be involved in the onset of diabetes mellitus

TYPES OF FATS	
Kind of fatty acid	Examples
Saturated H H H H | | | | H–C–C–C–C–H | | | | H H H H	Butter Cheese Chocolate Coconut and coconut oil Egg yolk Lard/Animal fat Meat Milk Palm oil Poultry Vegetable shortening
Monounsaturated H H H H H H | | | | | | H–C–C–C = C–C–C–H | | | | H H H H	Avocado Cashews Olives and olive oil Peanuts and peanut oil Peanut butter
Polyunsaturated H H H H H H H | | | | | | | H–C–C = C–C–C = C–C–H | | | H H H	Almonds Corn oil Cottonseed oil Filberts Fish Margarine (most) Mayonnaise Pecans Safflower oil Salad dressing Soybean oil Walnuts

C, a carbon atom.   −, a single bond.
H, a hydrogen atom.   =, a double bond.

(commonly known just as diabetes), and that diets lacking in fiber can also cause intestinal problems, such as constipation. (Fiber is found in coarse or bulky food, such as bran, that is high in indigestible plant material and low in nutrients but aids the body in ridding itself of solid waste material.) According to Michael Jacobson, these intestinal problems, in turn, help to support a $400 million laxative industry in the United States.

The way Americans eat, combined with a lack of exercise, also causes many people to become overweight. In fact, according to Jacobson, 14% of adult men and 24% of adult women are at least 20% above their desirable weight. That means that nearly 1 out of every 4 women who should weigh 125 pounds weighs 150 or more.

In 1977 the U.S. Senate Committee on Nutrition and Human Needs, after listening to the testimony of physicians and other nutritional experts on the American diet, recommended a 25% reduction in consumption of fat, a 50% to 85% reduction in sodium intake, and a 40% reduction in consumpton of refined sugar, the type found in cookies and candy. The committee also recommended that Americans double their consumption of starchy (fibrous) foods, such as potatoes and whole grain breads.

Many Americans found these Senate Committee suggestions very hard to implement. Consequently, in 1980, the U.S. Department of Agriculture and the U.S. Department of Health and Human Services released seven simplified "Dietary Guidelines for Americans," which consist of the following:

1. Eat a variety of foods.

2. Maintain ideal weight.

3. Avoid too much fat, cholesterol, and saturated fat (which includes animal fat and some vegetable fats such as those from coconut and palm oils, which are used in many commercially prepared baked goods; saturated fat has been shown to be a factor in causing the conditions that lead to heart disease).

4. Eat foods with adequate starch and fiber.

5. Avoid too much sugar.

6. Avoid too much sodium.

7. If you drink alcohol, do so in moderation.

In light of all the new information uncovered about nutrition since 1980, the University of Wisconsin Hospital and Clinics has added the following three guidelines:

1. Eat a moderate amount of polyunsaturated fat, such as corn, soy, safflower, sunflower, or olive oils and corn oil margarine, which has been shown to help lower cholesterol in the blood (high cholesterol can lead to heart disease).

2. Drink only a moderate amount of caffeine—caffeine is found in coffee and tea and in many cola soft drinks—in excess it may cause cystic breast disease (a condition in which breasts may tend to develop cysts, which are abnormal closed sacs).

3. Eat adequate amounts of calcium, which helps keep bones strong, and potassium, which counteracts sodium's ability to regulate blood pressure. Calcium is found in milk products and dark green vegetables. Potassium is present in fruits and vegetables, especially bananas and dried figs.

Reducing Fat Intake

Perhaps the most important of all the suggested guidelines is the one that calls for a reduction in fat intake. This is because high-fat diets promote heart disease and cancers of the breast, colon (the bottom part of the large intestine), and prostate (a gland in men surrounding the neck of the bladder). These diseases account for about 800,000 deaths each year in the United States alone.

Most Americans should reduce the percentage of fat in their diets from 40% to 25%. The following is a list of suggestions that, if followed, will help to reduce fat intake:

1. Drink skim milk or low-fat (1%) milk.

2. Instead of relying on meat as a source of protein, eat beans, pasta, rice, potatoes, and other starchy foods, as well as low-fat cottage cheese, fish, and chicken without the skin.

3. Avoid hot dogs, bologna, and processed luncheon meats since they get 80% of their calories from fat.

4. Trim as much visible fat as possible from meat, both before it is cooked and after it is on the dinner plate.

5. Use a lower grade of meat. The higher, more expensive grades, labeled "choice" and "prime," are higher in fat than the "good" grade, which has a perfectly acceptable taste for soups and stews. Look for new, low-fat beef in the grocery store.

6. When looking for something to put on bread pass by the butter, margarine, and cream cheese and instead choose honey, jam, or apple butter or eat the bread plain.

7. Make a snack out of fresh fruit, low-fat frozen yogurt, or ice milk instead of ice cream, pastries, or doughnuts.

8. Poach, steam, or roast meat, fish, and poultry instead of frying them, which requires the use of fat.

Knowing What One Is Eating

Following these guidelines is easier if one knows what one is eating. Many restaurants do not make nutritional information available, although more and more are offering healthy or diet choices. As for store-bought foods, most packaged products give a list of ingredients, and many include a nutritional breakdown of such important elements as calories, cholesterol, and sodium. The ingredients must be listed in order of quantity with the primary ingredient listed first and the one used in the smallest amount listed last. If a cereal's list of ingredients starts off, "wheat, corn, sugar," wheat is more predominant than corn or sugar, and sugar most likely constitutes less than one third of the product.

If a food makes a nutritional claim, such as "high in vitamin C" or "low in fat," then its label must include the following: serving size; servings per container; calories; protein, carbohydrate, fat, and sodium content, usually listed in grams; and several vitamins, usually listed as percentages of the U.S. Recommended Daily Allowance (USRDA).

Eating Habits

In order to adopt a truly health-conscious diet, Americans need to become more aware of how they eat. Long gone are the days

Most Americans need to eat less fat (especially cholesterol), sodium, and sugar, and to exercise more.

when every family ate three planned meals together. In their place, often, are microwave dinners, freeze-dried foods, and take-out. Pillsbury, the company known for its baked goods and also the parent company of the Burger King and Godfather Pizza fast-food chains, conducted a study that traced changes in American eating habits from 1971 to 1986. The study found that family dinners have declined sharply and that more Americans were eating fast foods.

The smallest segment in the study, 15% of the U.S. population, according to Pillsbury, was composed of the people who cooked from scratch and served their families homemade dinners and baked goods. The largest group, on the other hand, was what Pillsbury referred to as the "Chase and Grabbits." This group, an astonishing 26% of the population, consisted of people who lived on fast food, frozen dinners, and pizza. One bright point in the survey was that "careful cooks," or those who are health-conscious and whose cooking reflects their awareness of health issues, grew by 122%; this group now makes up 20% of the population. Unfortunately, the people in this group are more likely to be older and retired, so it is unlikely that they are cooking for a family and passing on their nutritional values to the next generations.

For the most part, eating healthily is not easy at first, but once a person begins consciously keeping track of all the foods he or she eats and begins substituting healthy foods for potentially harmful ones, the task becomes much easier. In the long run, of course, the payoff is a healthier body and a longer life.

For most people, adjusting eating habits and practicing good nutrition may be difficult, but it is not impossible. Usually, people take in enough food to keep their body functioning adequately, if not perfectly. Some people, however, do not take in enough food, take in too much food and then forcefully rid their body of it, or simply take in far too much. These people are said to be suffering from eating disorders. The next chapter will take a look at the history of weight and body ideals.

•   •   •   •

CHAPTER 2

· · · · · · · · · · · · · ·

THE HISTORY
OF EATING
DISORDERS

A Roman feast.

The ancient Egyptians believed in regular monthly purges to avoid illness. During the 1st century A.D., the ancient Romans invented the vomitorium, where men could empty out their stomachs after overindulging at a heavy banquet and return to eat more. The first recorded instances of an illness resembling anorexia (a disease characterized by self-starvation), however, did not appear until the Middle Ages.

Although *anorexia mirabilis* (miraculous lack of appetite), as it was known, is considered by some to be the forerunner of

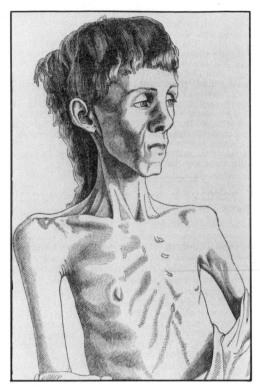

Nineteenth-century British physician William Gull proposed forced feeding, "moral" teaching, and a change of scene as treatment for anorexia. The drawings above, which appeared in the journal Lancet *in 1888, are before-and-after drawings of a young anorexic cured by Gull.*

today's anorexia nervosa, the phenomenon is actually quite different. As Dr. Joan Jacobs Brumberg points out in her book *Fasting Girls*, the earlier preoccupation with food denial reflected the cultural values of a period when the ideal was to be perfectly devout. That preoccupation represented perfection in terms of spiritual beauty, whereas modern anorexia nervosa expresses an individual's striving for today's ideal of perfection: physical beauty.

It was not until 1873 that two doctors, one English and one French, began to describe the disorder as it is known today. Sir William Gull, a practitioner and a physician to England's royal family, named the malady and described it for the first time as a separate disease—different from hysteria or biological eating problems. Before this, self-starvation had been considered an outgrowth either of insanity or of organic diseases such as tuberculosis, diabetes, and cancer. Although Gull felt that the illness arose from a diseased mental state, he did not recommend that his patients, almost all of whom were from the wealthier social classes in England, be institutionalized as the insane were. Instead, Gull saw anorexics as displaying a "perversion of the will" which expressed their "restless and wayward" natures. He treated the young women who came to him by prescribing forced feeding, "moral" teaching, and a change of scene.

Across the English Channel in Paris, Charles Lasegue, a French psychiatrist, described anorexia from a social and psychological standpoint. Lasegue believed that anorexia was a disease that could develop only in comfortable homes with an abundance of food and a pattern of well-regulated mealtimes. At these meals, manners, which required that children eat everything on their plate, were stressed and enforced. Naturally, this made mealtimes stressful and led some children to refuse to eat as a form of rebellion.

Another social and economic condition that may have contributed to the development of the disease was the expectation that girls remain at home after childhood, neither working nor going to school. Their "work" was to conduct a social life that would lead to a marriage that would in turn enhance the family's social status. In this endeavor, the girl's feelings were not very important. Life in such family situations was often suffocating for these young women, yet emotional outbursts such as temper tantrums were not allowed. By not eating, a young woman was protesting with semi-acceptable passive behavior, which, when she became ill and emaciated, made her the center of a tremendous amount of concern within her family—attention that she grew accustomed to and enjoyed.

According to Brumberg, it took a Frenchman, entrenched in that country's fascination with cuisine, to see the connection between love and food and thus to diagnose anorexia as a problem of conflict within families. It had been speculated by Lasegue that for these girls, rejecting food was a rejection of the parental love that they found both suffocating and manipulative.

Since 1873, doctors have agreed on the medical characteristics of anorexia: lack of appetite, emaciation, cessation of menstruation (for females), low body temperature, and hyperactivity. In

A 19th-century advertisement for Coraline corsets. Throughout the centuries, women have sought methods and devices for making themselves appear thinner. The corset, an undergarment designed to suppress the waist, was one such device.

the early period after its "discovery," most also agreed that the patient refused to eat in order to attract attention.

Another possible cause was advanced by Silas Weir Mitchell (1829–1914), a prominent American neurologist, who instead saw anorexia nervosa as a variant of *neurasthenia*, an organic nervous disorder characterized by nervous exhaustion and a lack of motivation. Mitchell thought the disease was precipitated by any stressful life event in combination with the new, late-19th-century social pressures on women (including higher education and new opportunities for social participation).

The prescribed treatment for anorexia at that time was removal from the family home, called a "parentectomy" by Gull, and forced feeding by whatever means necessary. At the turn of the century, the newest, most scientific treatment was the "Mitchell Method," devised by Silas Mitchell, which prescribed bed rest, total seclusion, a diet low in fats, and massage. This regimen, Mitchell said, would lead to recovery for that class of "thin-blooded emotional women" who made poor health a "cherished habit."

Refusing food because of social pressures was in keeping with

Victorian ideals. In the second half of the 19th century, it was common for young women and girls to skip meals and restrict their intake of certain foods, particularly meat. A hearty appetite was said to represent sexuality and lack of self-restraint, and women were expected to be passive and uninterested in both sex and food. Also, many people living during the Victorian era emphasized spirituality and, as evidence of their pursuit of spiritual rather than material interests, a thin body. As a result of the heavy (meat and potatoes, an abundance of starches), multi-course meals that were the norm at the time, however, many women were actually quite large.

By 1899, when the American economist Thorstein Veblen published his influential book *The Theory of the Leisure Class*, thinness meant its possessor could afford to be idle. Thinness was therefore socially desirable to the upper class, just as robust health was considered a mark of the lower classes. Thus, morally, spiritually, and socially it was considered desirable for Victorian women to refuse food, even before the dictates of 20th century fashion and advertising.

In 1906, Pierre Janet, an important French psychiatrist, spoke about anorexia at Harvard Medical School. He agreed with Viennese psychoanalyst Sigmund Freud, who believed that it was the physical manifestation of an emotional, possibly sexual, conflict. But Janet said that he viewed this refusal to eat not as a matter of appetite or control of appetite, but rather as an obsession with many possible sources, including the Victorian ideals of spirituality. Janet also felt that the desire to starve oneself could come from a deep sense of shame about the body that made eating seem immoral.

Thus, as the 20th century began, two pioneers of psychotherapy were linking anorexia to the desire to retard normal sexual development. Yet it was not until the late 1930s, when psychiatry became more generally accepted, that these ideas were incorporated into the treatment of anorexia.

By the 1930s there was a new interest in the connections between mind and body, as reflected by the growth in *psychosomatic medicine* (a branch of medicine dealing with the interconnection between the mind and the body) and psychosomatic diseases. During the 1930s, doctors began to believe that permanent recovery from anorexia required not only weight gain but also exploration of the psychological basis of the disorder. To achieve this goal, the patient underwent classic psychoanalysis to help him or her understand the experiences or ideals that led him or her to refuse food. This discovery and understanding, the doctors believed, took place over a long period of time and after a number of interviews with a psychoanalyst, who was mostly a passive listener and infrequent questioner.

By the 1940s psychiatrists of certain schools of thought were convinced that female anorexics feared that eating would lead to oral impregnation, with obesity being viewed as a sort of pregnancy. Thus, the search for oral impregnation fantasies dominated therapeutic sessions during those years. At this time, some schizophrenics were diagnosed as being anorexic as well, leading to the inclusion of delusions (false beliefs about people or oneself with no basis in reality) and hallucinations (seeing or perceiving in some way something that is not there) as symptoms of anorexia.

Although anorexia was increasingly recognized in the medical world as a disease, it was Dr. Hilde Bruch who really brought the disease to light. Trained as a pediatrician specializing in physiological research in Germany in the late 1920s and early 1930s, Dr. Bruch left Germany for England when Hitler came to power in 1933. There she worked in a child guidance clinic for a year before moving to the United States. In the United States, working and studying at the medical schools of both Columbia and Johns Hopkins Universities, she became an expert on childhood obesity. Then, because of her discovery that deficient mother-child relationships were at the root of the obesity, she decided to become a psychiatrist.

Dr. Bruch first wrote on anorexia in 1961, but it was her 1973 book *Eating Disorders: Obesity, Anorexia Nervosa, and the Person Within* that brought eating disorders to national attention. Dr. Bruch, who did most of her work on anorexia at Baylor University Medical School in Houston, Texas, saw the "relentless pursuit of thinness" as the outstanding symptom of anorexia. She also described anorexics as having severe body-image disturbances that made them unable to accurately identify their own emotions and such bodily sensations as hunger. Bruch also characterized anorexics as having the sort of black-and-white, or concrete, thinking typical of much younger children. This meant that they thought that things were good or bad, right or wrong, with no shades of meaning in between. Finally, she saw anorexics as suffering from a pervasive sense of ineffectiveness—in both personal relationships and in life in general. In effect, Bruch saw what many earlier doctors had ignored: that anorexia was a mental disorder.

Since Bruch's first article, others have had ideas that either coexist or conflict slightly with hers. These ideas have not only expanded the current understanding of anorexia but they have also led to successful experimentation leading to improved research and treatment.

In 1975, Salvador Minuchin, a psychiatrist at the University of Pennsylvania, proposed that anorexia was caused by families that did not allow the anorexic to develop the autonomy he or she was expected to display at the time of adolescence. This thinking led to the development of family therapy for anorexia, a treatment method that will be discussed in Chapter 7.

In 1982, scientists at the Royal Edinburgh Hospital and the Royal Infirmary in England put forth a theory that anorexia actually had a physical basis. Their theory, based on studies they had conducted on 10 anorexics and 12 normal volunteers, supported many anorexics' claims that they felt full even hours after eating. The doctors suggested that the reason was that the rate at which anorexics' digestive systems emptied was different from the normal people's rate. To prove this, they tagged the solid and liquid parts of the meals fed to the test subjects and measured both amount and time elapsed as the matter was excreted. The results showed that although there was no difference in the rate at which their stomachs emptied in the early part of digestion, after 10 minutes the digestive systems of the anorexics slowed drastically.

The researchers speculated that this slowdown was hormonal, related to the *hypothalamus* (a section of the brain responsible for food intake). This hypothesis has further support in that the majority of anorexics are women with abnormal menstrual cycles (this abnormality can also be caused by a hormone imbalance) and that they are more likely to be young, often just entering puberty and experiencing drastic hormonal changes. The search for a possible biological/hormonal cause for anorexia continues today.

According to the *Diagnostic and Statistical Manual of Mental Disorders*, Third Edition (DSM-III), published by the American Psychiatric Association, the changes in criteria for anorexia from 1980 to 1987 were relatively minor. The major change was a matter of degree: In 1987 the weight loss that defined the anorexic condition was reduced from 25% to 15% of normal body weight. The new definition added the "absence of at least three consecutive menstrual periods when otherwise expected to occur." Menstruation had not been mentioned in 1980.

In Hilde Bruch's last book, *Conversations with Anorexics*, published posthumously in 1988 (she died in 1984) with the help of two of her colleagues, Bruch altered slightly her formulation of what anorexia meant. She saw the "disturbed body image, confusion about body sensations, and an all-pervasive sense of ineffectiveness . . . as an expression of defective self-concept, concealed under all circumstances." She wrote of the anorexic that "all her efforts, her striving for perfection and excessive thinness, are directed toward hiding the fatal flaw of her fundamental inadequacy."

THE HISTORY OF BULIMIA

In tracing the history of bulimia (a disease characterized by periods of binging followed by periods of purging) in *The Psychiatric Clinics of North America 1964*, Craig Johnson, M.D., codirector of the eating-disorders program at Northwestern University Medical School and a major researcher on bulimia, pointed out that although bulimic behavior was described in the late 19th century, the disorder did not receive serious attention until the 1940s, when it was considered a symptom of anorexia. Bulimia among people without histories of weight disorders was first described in 1976 by Drs. M. Boskind-White and W. C. White, Jr., who coined the term "bulimarexia."

In 1979, London doctor G. F. M. Russell was the first physician to describe bulimia as a disease different from anorexia and to give it a name. He called the disease *bulimia nervosa* to stress his thinking that it was a variant of anorexia, and he described it in the following way: "The patient suffers from powerful and intractable urges to overeat; the patient seeks to avoid the 'fattening' effects of food by inducing vomiting or abusing purgatives or both; the patient has a morbid fear of becoming obese."

The following year bulimia nervosa appeared for the first time in the DSM. Changes in the criteria for diagnosis of bulimia between 1980 and 1987 give an idea of the changes in thinking about this disorder during this period. The 1980 criteria included full accounts of the binges, including their duration—"usually less than two hours at a time"—and the "inconspicuous eating" of "high caloric, easily ingested food." These binges were terminated by "sleep, abdominal pain, social interruption, or self-induced vomiting" and were followed by "depressed mood and self-deprecating thoughts." All of these symptoms (except the reference to vomiting), in addition to the assertion that "bulimic episodes are not due to anorexia or any known physical disorder," were removed in the 1987 edition of the DSM-III.

The emphasis in 1987 was on the frequency (at least twice a week) and length (at least three months) of the binging behavior, as opposed to what it looked or felt like. There was also an emphasis on the variety of ways—self-induced vomiting, use of lax-

A detail from Toilette de Venus, by the 17th-century Flemish painter Peter Paul Rubens. During the 17th century the ideal woman was buxom and well-rounded.

atives or diuretics, strict dieting or fasting, or vigorous exercise—used to rid the body of the calories ingested during a binge. These changes prevented the occasional binger from being classified as bulimic. They also brought anorexia and bulimia closer together, as "strict dieting or fasting" and "persistent overconcern with body shape and weight" were added to the purging behaviors. This made it possible to see the relationship between the problems of a normal-weight bulimic and those of a severely emaciated anorexic.

TWENTIETH-CENTURY SOCIETY

Society and its prevalent attitudes have probably contributed to the development of anorexia and other eating disorders. Before the 20th century, and in many cultures around the world today, the ideal female figure was, and is, "pleasantly plump." Indeed, much of the world's great art—the 17th-century paintings of Peter Paul Rubens (1577–1640), to take just one example—features buxom, well-rounded women. This roundness was believed to show that a woman would be good at bearing and rearing children and, in cultures where food was scarce, that she had enough to eat.

At the beginning of the 20th century, however, perceptions began to change. American women, who fought for and, in 1920, won the right to vote, were also beginning to work outside the home. In the male-dominated arena of work, it was considered helpful for a woman to have a "less-womanly" and "more-masculine" body, in order to fit in and be taken more seriously.

At the same time, the newly developing fashion industry, taking its cue from the Paris designer Paul Poiret, who emphasized a lean silhouette, was turning out clothes geared to thin models. Until the first quarter of the 20th century, clothing was made at home or by a family seamstress; there were few stores selling clothes of different styles and sizes, all made up and "ready to wear." (For the most part, clothes were custom made for the very wealthy from different models or simply homemade by the less well-to-do). Although the new industry brought convenience, it also brought with it standard sizes. Before, the dress had been made to fit the body; now the body had to fit the dress.

In the 1920s, thinness became even more of an ideal for

During the 1920s slenderness was in vogue and the "flapper" (a young woman sporting short hair and a short dress) was the feminine ideal.

women; indeed, thinness was considered sexy. Because it was the opposite of the plump, maternal, tied-to-home-and-family figure, thin came to mean free and available. The desired look was exemplified by the flapper of the Roaring Twenties who, in a first for women, wore both her hair and her skirt short. (Flappers' skirts stopped at the knee; previously, skirts had reached to the ankle.) The 1920s also witnessed an increase in the social acceptability of divorce; contemporary magazines responded by advertising slenderness as a way to hold on to a husband.

During the Great Depression of the 1930s, when many people were truly worried about getting enough to eat, and the early 1940s, when national attention was focused on winning World War II, the emphasis on thinness was less intense. But after the war the message again came across loud and clear, only this time directed at teenagers as well as at their mothers and older sisters. *Seventeen* magazine, which had started publication in 1944 with articles on nutrition, had, by 1948, added articles on dieting and the importance of looking attractive.

However, the true obsession with extreme thinness can be

dated to the early 1960s. David M. Garner, Ph.D., and Dr. Paul E. Garfinkel, both of the University of Toronto, and historians D. Schwartz and M. Thompson studied *Playboy* magazine centerfolds and Miss America pageants from 1959 to 1978 and noticed some interesting trends. First, women chosen to exemplify both sexual and fashionable beauty consistently weighed less than the amount recommended in the standard weight tables issued by life insurance companies. Second, both the *Playboy* models and the Miss America contestants became progressively thinner during the period studied. Interestingly, at this time the average weight of women under 30 was increasing steadily. Nevertheless, the wish to be thinner was well on its way to becoming a preoccupation among American women.

Contemporary Statistics

Contemporary figures on the prevalence of eating disorders vary greatly. One problem is that so many of those who suffer keep their illness private. Another is that the severity of symptoms varies, so it is not always easy to know who to count. According

The British model Twiggy was the super-thin ideal of the 1960s.

A 19-year study concerning women who compete in beauty pageants and those who appear in Playboy magazine showed that women who are considered to exemplify sexual and fashionable beauty weigh less than the weights recommended by life-insurance tables.

to Dr. Garfinkel, 90% to 95% of those who suffer from eating disorders are female. For anorexic teenage girls the numbers vary from 1 out of 250 to 1 out of 100 to many more than that in teenagers with some symptoms of an eating disorder.

Although someone who binges or purges occasionally would probably not be diagnosed as having an eating disorder, it seems clear that all of the studies indicate that there is a large number of young people, especially women, who are preoccupied with eating or, conversely, with thinness. Some scientists, including Dr. Garfinkel, feel that the blame for this unhealthy obsession may lie in the very fabric of society itself.

CONTEMPORARY CAUSES OF EATING DISORDERS

Social scientists, historians, and physicians seeking to explain why so many individuals in our society are suffering from eating disorders focus on three main areas: society, and specifically the role of women in society; the psychological makeup and family interactions of individual patients; and biological abnormalities.

Those who look at society almost always point to its obsession with thinness for women. Whereas men are valued for what they do, which often means what they have accomplished in work or at school, women are often valued—and, most important and most dangerous, sometimes value themselves—on the basis of their looks.

This preoccupation with thinness starts early and continues into old age. Another study of teenage girls, conducted by Dr. William Feldman at the University of Ottawa, found that 50% thought they were too fat even though only 17% were actually overweight. With the preference for thinness comes, not surprisingly, unfair prejudice against obesity. Children as young as six, when shown silhouettes of an obese child, describe the child as "lazy, dirty, stupid, and ugly."

Tragically, the worries do not end as women get older, when one might expect them to worry less about their figure. Very often, the obsession with dieting and thinness carries through until the end of a woman's life, or at least into old age. In the next chapter the obsession with dieting will be explored, as well as the tools, legitimate or otherwise, that many people use to attain their weight goals.

•　　　•　　　•　　　•

CHAPTER 3

DRUGS AND WEIGHT-LOSS PROGRAMS

At this very moment, millions of people the world over are trying to lose weight. According to a September 7, 1986, article by N. R. Kleinfeld that appeared in the *New York Times*, Americans alone spend billions of dollars a year on diet and exercise programs. This figure includes almost a billion dollars for diet meals and food substitutes, and close to $200 million for nonprescription diet pills.

Sadly, many of these products either do not work, or they endanger the life of those who rely upon them. Many diet programs work for a while, but eventually the dieter regains all the weight lost. In many cases, this is not the programs' fault. As anyone who has been on a diet knows, taking off the pounds—and keeping them off—is not easy. For this reason, many dieters experience the "yo-yo" syndrome—gaining weight, losing it, and then putting it back on again. In some cases, this pattern can last a lifetime.

Although many people lose weight by reducing the number of calories they take in and increasing the amount of time they exercise, others rely on different means to help them lose weight. Diet drugs—sold over the counter as "candies" or tablets—are a popular, albeit dangerous, choice. Most diet pills available on the market today are appetite suppressants—they keep the dieter from feeling hungry. Most also contain the active ingredient *phenylpropanolamine* (PPA—a nasal decongestant), in addition to caffeine and fiber, gels, or another base. The potential side effects of diet pills, however, far outweigh their use as a diet aid. Side effects include increase in blood pressure, erratic heartbeat, dizziness, irritability, nausea, nervousness, insomnia, rapid pulse, and tightness in the chest. In addition, people with diabetes, kidney problems, high blood pressure, or thyroid disorders should never take any drug containing PPA, for they are more likely to have severe side effects. Physicians also feel that people under the age of 18 should refrain from taking these and any other over-the-counter medications without consulting their physician first.

The risk of taking over-the-counter medications is compounded by the fact that people often tailor the drug to fit their diet plan. This may mean that if dieters feel that they are losing weight too slowly on two pills a day, they may increase the dosage to four pills a day, thus increasing their chances of dangerous side effects and possible overdose.

Diuretics—chemicals that lessen the amount of fluids in the body—are also often used as a diet tool. Unfortunately, diuretics remove not only water from the body but also important minerals such as sodium. Side effects of diuretics include: loss of skin elasticity, loss of pressure in eyeballs, dry tongue, decrease in blood volume, low blood pressure, fainting, and, in extreme cases, kidney failure, heart attack, and even death.

Diet aids, or drugs used to induce weight loss, can have serious side effects such as irritability and increased heart rate.

Laxatives are chemicals that rid the body of wastes that accumulate in the large intestine. The chemicals loosen and add bulk to the waste material, which then irritates or stimulates the large intestine. Prescribed by doctors for certain exams, or before surgery, laxatives are also available over the counter for home use. Many dieters, however, use laxatives to rid themselves of unwanted food, or to relieve themselves of the feeling of fullness. Continued use, however, can lead to cramping, diarrhea, and improper absorption of nutrients. With prolonged use, and in extreme cases, laxatives can lead to extended bouts of diarrhea which, in turn, can lead to significant vitamin and mineral loss and an imbalance in the body's *electrolytes* (substances within the body that conduct electricity through the movement of ions). Laxatives can also lead to dehydration and, in severe cases, to exhaustion and unconsciousness.

DIET PROGRAMS

The 20th century has witnessed a plethora of books and magazine articles touting one diet or another as the cure to weight gain. There has been the Scarsdale diet, the watermelon diet, and the carbohydrate diet, just to name a few. Each has enjoyed its time in the limelight, and each has, likewise, failed to live up to its promise of being the miracle weight-loss diet. Most of these "fad" diets enjoy their moment of fame and then simply fade away when their promises are not kept. Others, however, are dangerous and encourage dieters to eat all of one type of food and to give up all others—to eat only proteins, for example. As will be discussed further on in this volume, weight-loss programs such as these can lead to serious health risks and, in some cases, death.

There are, however, several diet programs that are nationally known and have offered help to dieters throughout the country.

Weight Watchers

Considered by many health-care professionals to be one of the very best weight-loss programs, Weight Watchers has thousands

A mother and son hold up pants they used to wear before they joined Weight Watchers and lost more than 100 pounds each. The Weight Watchers program entails weekly meetings and planned meals.

of centers nationwide. The program consists of a weekly weigh-in, followed by a short lecture and a question-and-answer, or open discussion, period. The diet itself is broken down into servings of fruits and vegetables, proteins, carbohydrates, and fats, with the dieter allowed to choose a certain number of servings from each group to make up meals and snacks for the day. As the weeks progress, the dieter is given a broader list to choose from and additional calories to "spend" on snacks.

Weight Watchers does have its own line of foods, available in supermarkets nationwide, and its own magazine as well. The foods are not required eating, however, as part of the diet program. After losing the desired amount of weight (determined by the dieter in consultation with the program leader), the member is put on the maintenance program. If the member maintains his or her weight for six weeks or more, he or she becomes a lifetime member and must attend only one meeting a month and must not go more than two pounds above goal weight. The start-up or registration fee for the program ranges from $20 to $30, depending upon location, and costs either $8 or $9 a week.

Optifast and Other Fasting Programs

Optifast, much like Medifast and a number of other fasting programs nationwide, is a physician-supervised program of weight loss specially designed for those people with a large amount of weight to lose. Before beginning the program, dieters are required to undergo blood tests, a complete physical, and an *electrocardiogram* (EKG). This is mainly because the program requires abstinence from solid foods—fasting—and allows members to drink only specially formulated powdered drinks. This fasting can lead to hair loss and, in some cases, heart attack and stroke.

The program itself involves weekly weigh-ins and lectures. The start-up cost is quite high—$100 or more for the physical and tests, and $50 to $100 a week depending on the amount of weight to be lost. Some insurance companies, however, will cover the expenses. In recent years, some members of the medical profession have begun to question the safety and wisdom of such fasting programs.

Diet Center

Established in 1971 and including more than 2,300 centers nationwide, Diet Center requires more of an intensive commitment from its members. Members must come to the center five or six days a week to be weighed in, to go over food diaries, and to speak to a nutritionist. Foods are also available, manufactured by the program, at each center. These foods, like those of Weight Watchers, are not required for the program.

The start-up cost of the program is $100, with weekly costs running about $60, depending upon the desired weight loss. The maintenance program, which lasts one year, costs $300.

Nutrisystem

With over 1,000 centers in both the United States and Canada, Nutrisystem is a diet program centered on eating modification. The program, started in 1971, revolves around weekly weigh-ins and meetings with a nutritionist, followed by a lecture. At the initial consultation, which is free, the nutritionist with the help of a computer determines the dieter's ideal body weight and ideal speed of weight loss. The dieter is then presented with an individualized weight-loss plan. Nutrisystem members must purchase their food at the centers themselves. The cost for each program depends upon the individual case and program chosen.

The diet programs discussed in this book have been successful for a large number of people across the country. Not every diet is perfect for every dieter, however, nor is it safe. Before beginning any diet, the dieter should first consult a physician.

Many people neither consult a doctor nor join any of the above-mentioned programs. Some of these people start out dieting on their own, cutting their food allowance down each day until they are barely eating at all. These people are said to be suffering from an eating disorder. In the next chapter the disease anorexia will be discussed—a disease that often begins with chronic dieting.

•   •   •   •

CHAPTER 4

ANOREXIA

Although most people have an idea of what anorexia is all about—the starving, the denial, the compulsion—few probably truly understand what anorexia really involves. With each case of anorexia there is a different set of reasons, background circumstances, and habits.

To be able to distinguish an eating disorder, it is first necessary to look at the factors many of the cases have in common and then to look at individual cases and see how different people act while suffering from the disease. Each case of anorexia is different—each individual manifests symptoms of the disease in different ways. But it is possible to give a composite of what an anorexic's feelings, behavior, and eating habits might be. In this way, people may better understand the disease and be better prepared to recognize a potential or current anorexic and offer assistance.

ANOREXIA: TAKING CONTROL

Anorexia is a mental illness involving the fear of eating and gaining weight. Sufferers of anorexia quite simply starve themselves. The overwhelming majority of anorexics are young women, commonly in their early or late teens. The anorexic is usually conscientious in her schoolwork—a perfectionist. Inside, however, she does not feel good about herself and suffers from a lack of self-esteem. Male anorexics, as well, may feel insecure about themselves, particularly about their ability to attract members of the same or the opposite sex.

The anorexic's behavior does not usually begin as extraordinary dieting. Rather, in a young woman's case, it is often precipitated by a comment about her gaining weight, often made by her father, or it might begin with a startling view in the mirror

For some young girls, a close look in the mirror can be the event that triggers years of self-starvation.

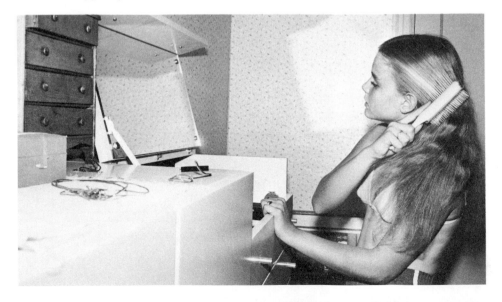

For most young women, puberty signals the onset of interest in the opposite sex. For some girls, however, fear of the sexual maturity and accompanying physical changes brought on by puberty activates the onset of anorexia.

of her more-womanly figure as she reaches puberty. It may also be caused by a traumatic life event—a divorce, a death in the family, breaking up with her boyfriend, or beginning college. Often the initial diet is timed to coincide with a point of change— such as starting at a new school—when the young woman may want to be thin so she will be accepted by her new classmates. For a young man, anorexia often develops as a result of a diet to overcome obesity or to make himself attractive to others. For both young men and women, however, anorexia may develop as part of an antiobesity campaign that is simply carried too far. Whether this campaign is brought on by societal pressures or is the result of the person's own fear, the result is the same: A dangerous eating disorder develops.

Another possible avenue leading to anorexia for young women is isolation and the fear of entering puberty or becoming sexually mature. In this case, the anorexic may become socially isolated the year before she begins starving herself, either dropping her friends or being dropped by them. She may become prudish and disapprove of friends who are interested in boys and parties, and she may say that no one she knows can live up to her standards.

The young woman decides that dieting will solve all of her

problems. Restricting what she is eating and losing weight will help her gain control over her life and help her to be a better person, she reasons. Then, what starts as a moderate diet develops into anorexia.

According to Dr. Jack Katz, clinical director of the Division of Acute Treatment Services at the Westchester Division of New York Hospital and clinical professor of psychiatry at Cornell University Medical College, a young woman may also slip into anorexia from less obvious causes. She may begin as a runner, for example, losing weight; beginning to like the new thinness, she may stop eating altogether. Or she may become ill with mononucleosis or some other sickness, suffer a large weight loss, and then become anorexic.

In this next stage, with a tremendous display of willpower the anorexic may enlarge the terms of her diet to include cutting out whole groups of food, such as carbohydrates and fats. She may also begin to skip meals.

Anorexics find ways to avoid eating—they are often late in the morning and skip breakfast, join sports activities and miss lunch, and make up excuses for not eating with the family. If an anorexic is forced to share a meal with other people, she will pick at her food or push it around the plate so that it looks like it has been eaten. Often, an anorexic will take little bites of a low-calorie food, such as an apple or a piece of lettuce, chewing it sometimes hundreds of times to delay swallowing.

Many anorexics feel full after a piece of lettuce or a single egg. Because most anorexics do not like the feeling of having food in their stomach, they refrain from drinking even diet soda or water, which may create a sensation of fullness. In extreme cases anorexics worry about gaining weight from gum, toothpaste, or cough drops, or even from licking the back of a stamp.

Some anorexics will insist upon eating dinner at a specific time each night and will not allow food to pass their lips past that time. Others will eat only from a specific plate and will insist upon eating foods only in special combinations or in a particular order.

In a recent interview, Dr. Judith Russkay Rabinor, a psychologist with a practice in Lido Beach, New York, pointed out that she has found that although all anorexics drastically restrict their food intake, they do not all do so in a similar pattern. One anorexic may eat raisins all day, while another may starve during the day and eat at night. Still other anorexics eat during the day and never at night or starve Monday through Friday and eat only on the weekends.

Dr. Hilde Bruch speculated that the transition from ordinary dieting to starvation dieting is not something that is planned. "Not one of the patients I have known," she wrote in *Eating Disorders: Obesity, Anorexia Nervosa, and the Person Within,* "had intended to pursue the frightening road of life-threatening emaciation." The crossover, however, may be prompted by the extra attention the young people receive for having so much willpower and for initially looking so good after a small reduction in weight. "The real difference," Bruch continued, "lies in the extraordinary pride and pleasure she takes in being able to do something so hard. Suddenly it is easy and the conviction comes that it can go on forever; and this quickly turns into the feeling of 'I enjoy being hungry.'"

The praise accompanying a healthy weight loss may make an adolescent whose family never seems to notice him or her feel good—may make an adolescent feel that he or she is finally receiving some attention. Tragically, despite their pride in their accomplishment and the discovery that they do have willpower, anorexics never think they are thin enough. They still look in the mirror and see unwanted flesh.

Even though they are starving themselves, anorexics are preoccupied with food. This may mean that they talk about food incessantly or read cookbooks from cover to cover. They may devise menus for their family and then insist upon doing the shopping, cooking, and serving—but never the eating.

Anorexics are also often fanatically active. They become relentless athletes, running 10 miles instead of 5 and following this with sit-ups and jumping jacks that they can do secretly in their room. It is not unusual for anorexics to set the alarm for 4:00 A.M. so that they can exercise for two hours before the rest of the family gets up. All of this activity, compounded by the lack of sleep and eating that often accompany it, reflects anorexics' desire to subjugate a body whose transformation into perfect thinness they think will magically solve all of their problems.

In the beginning, the discipline and manic activity are a source of pleasure to anorexics. They may be arrogant about all that

Anorexics often start out as normal athletes, such as the young girls shown here. Whereas most young girls will stop after one hour of practice, however, the anorexic may extend it to three or four hours—often exercising when no one else is around.

they have accomplished. As time passes, however, things begin to change. Anorexics becomes weak, their eyes look glazed, and they may find it difficult to concentrate at work or school. Anorexics soon have trouble sleeping even when sleep is desired, and the weight loss makes even normal activities such as sitting painful, as the body has lost its extra cushion of body fat.

Although anorexia does technically mean "lack of appetite," this definition is not completely accurate. There are times, in fact, when anorexics will give in and binge—purging themselves afterward. Most of the time, however, anorexics have themselves under tight control and resist their appetite.

Physically, the female anorexic's body undergoes a number of changes as her disease progresses. She may have to take large doses of laxatives to combat the constipation brought about as a result of the lack of fiber in her diet. Menstruation ceases as well. Cessation of menstruation usually occurs after a large weight loss and is a sign that something is going wrong with the body.

Although she weighs herself several times throughout the day and her body is emacicated, she will look in the mirror and see herself as being fat. This perception, however incorrect, keeps her on her starvation course. At about the time when menstruation ceases, however, there may be a marked change in her behavior. Periods of frenzied activity may alternate with periods of depression and crying fits. The anorexic may lose her ability to concentrate and may experience memory lapses. And while an anorexic may acknowledge these disturbances, she will refuse to accept that her dieting is at the root of them.

Because of her extreme thinness, the anorexic is always cold. She no longer has any body fat to insulate her, and her metabolism is slowed down considerably. In addition, a fine growth of hair covers her body—this is her body's way of adjusting to the lower temperature. Dehydration may leave the anorexic's skin dry and cracked or yellow from increased deposits of carotene. Because of an obvious lack of protein, vitamins, and minerals in her body, the anorexic begins to experience muscle cramps and her hair begins to fall out; the hair that remains becomes dull and stringy.

In addition to those biological changes listed above, the female anorexic's body may undergo any of the following changes:

1. Generalized fatigue, lethargy, and lack of energy.

2. Cessation of menstruation, loss of sexual desire, and, possibly, irreversible loss of the ability to bear children.

3. Pallor of the skin, skin becomes pale or grayish, then dark and scaly.

4. Cramping of the muscles, muscles eventually waste away, making all physical activity difficult.

5. Numbness or tingling sensations in the hands or feet.

6. Stomach bloating, constipation, and difficulty urinating; kidney and bladder infections and stones in the urinary tract may appear.

7. Periods of dizziness, light-headedness, and even amnesia.

8. Shrinkage of internal organs, which, depending on the intensity and duration of the anorexia, may be irreversible.

9. Kidney failure.

10. Heart failure.

Kidney and heart failure can, of course, be fatal. The heart, a muscle, needs potassium to beat normally. A shortage of potassium leads the heart to beat more slowly and, eventually, to beat irregularly or to stop completely.

MADELYN'S STORY

In a 1988 interview, Madelyn, now a grown woman, related her battle with an eating disorder.

When I was 12 I put myself on a diet. I would drink one glass of powdered skim milk and eat one hard-boiled egg. I would eat an egg because that was a measured amount, and I used to agonize over the size of the egg after a while. I stayed on that diet for a month and a half—it was my secret. I got a baby-sitting job after school just so that I would not have to eat with my family. If I was not baby-sitting, I was at the library.

I was up all night exercising. I would wear layers of clothes so no one had any idea of what I was doing. If anyone said I looked drawn, haggard, or pale I would redouble my attempts to appear normal, all the time keeping to my 150-calorie-a-day diet. The next 20 years I spent trying to follow that diet and regain the feeling of control I had while on it.

One night I was dragged to a relative's house for dinner. I remember eating a piece of lettuce and feeling that the whole month and a half was for nothing, that my diet had been ruined. I wanted to kill myself. I felt very out of control. Later I realized that I thought then that my body and what I ate was the only thing I could control, and I was very good at that. As a typical perfectionist I did not want to do what I was not good at.

I forced myself to throw up because all this bad food was inside my body and it was poisoning me and making me fat. It would not have mattered if I had eaten something with little or no calories—the point was I did not want to feel full. I wanted to feel flat. If I drank water I was terrified that I was fat because my stomach stuck out a little.

The thinner I got the more obsessed I became with finding new places where I had fat, which I now realize was only skin. At that time I was just developing breasts and hips. I had just gotten my period, and the terror of my body changing and becoming even bigger—I was already bigger than the girls my age and that realization had helped trigger my diet—was horrible. Older men would react to me as if I were a woman when I was 12 or 13, and I was terrified. I spent a lot of time trying to reverse the years physically.

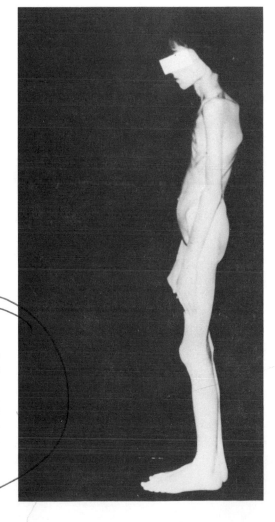

The physical effects of anorexia include loss of menstruation; dry, cracked skin; the sensation of extreme cold; dull hair; and loss of body fat as a cushion for organs and bones.

61

The effects of anorexia include decreased metabolism, shrinking of internal organs, and dry, scaly skin.

Weight was the whole focus of my life. I had been aware of it even before I began dieting. My older sister was very overweight and usually left the dinner table in tears. I felt very guilty about it, but I remember thinking I was glad I had an older sister like her so I would know I should never become that fat, that it was too painful. My older sister had no friends and was ridiculed by my father.

In eighth grade I started experimenting with speed and other drugs. I was never really an addict but I liked the drugs because they helped me keep my weight down. I went through high school wearing my coat and a few times was almost thrown out for refusing to take it off. I still got straight A's. I had two friends, a girlfriend and a boyfriend. I spent every day and night with these two people. They were the only people I trusted, but neither knew anything about my eating disorder, my horrible secret. By that time I was throwing up regularly, too. My whole life was based on how I looked physically; smartness fell by the wayside. Unfortunately, a large part of my new image was my sexiness, and deep down I knew that throwing up was not sexy.

Even though I was praised for my looks, I thought it was all because I was such a master of illusion. I felt that if anybody could really see me they would realize that I was not really thin or pretty enough.

After high school Madelyn attended college, graduated, and became engaged. A short while later she broke off the engagement and began traveling through the United States as well as going abroad. To support her drug and alcohol habits, she worked at menial jobs and lived with men who could give her what she craved and what they, too, were addicted to. Madelyn eventually married a known drug addict; they soon separated. Shortly after, she became very ill and entered a residential treatment program for eating disorders. At the treatment center she was in both individual and group psychotherapy. After a short time, however, she left the program. Throughout the entire 20-year period beginning when she was 12 and continuing until she was nearly 33, Madelyn starved, binged, and purged, all the time worrying that she might become fat.

Although Madelyn had realized that she had an eating disorder before she entered college, she was unsure of where to go to receive help. At that time, eating disorders were virtually unheard of (this was prior to the media blitz that followed), and barely understood. Consequently, Madelyn entered college, hoping that communal living situations, such as being in a dormitory or living with her boyfriend, would force her to change her eating behavior. Unfortunately, they never did.

Countless times Madelyn tried to stop binging and purging, only to find herself succumbing again. Finally, she gained control of her eating disorder by joining Overeaters Anonymous, a program that will be described in greater detail in Chapter 8. Overeaters Anonymous believes that its members must avoid pressuring themselves and, instead, focus on living without the abused substance (in this case food) "one day at a time." Madelyn points out that although she is now eating normal meals on most days, she is living her life "one meal at a time, and sometimes even one minute at a time."

•   •   •   •

CHAPTER 5
· · · · · · · · · · · · · · · · · ·

BULIMIA AND COMPULSIVE OVEREATING

Bulimia is an eating disorder that differs from anorexia in that sufferers continually binge—eat large amounts of food—and then purge themselves afterward. The purging is usually done by forcing oneself to throw up or, less commonly, by using laxatives and diuretics. Emotionally, bulimics may be repressing a great deal of anger, insecurity, and anxiety. In addition, they may be perfectionists. Many bulimics are depressed and suffer from an inability to deal with stress.

cause

Sufferers of bulimia binge and purge for a variety of reasons. Some bulimics binge only to be able to purge themselves afterward—it is the purge, in fact, that offers these people the most relief from their emotional distress. Other sufferers, however, crave the binge—they feel they *need* the food—and it is only the purge that allows them to have the binge without gaining weight.

The binge/purge syndrome usually begins as a response to overwhelming hunger brought on either by anorexia or by continual dieting. Once they discover that they can eat even more food than they want and not gain weight, they may become caught in the binge/purge trap. From that point on, whenever bulimics feel anxious or angry, or whenever they are faced with solitary, unplanned blocks of time, the binge/purge cycle may begin again. Bulimics, however, do not eat only in their spare time. They make time to eat and usually do their eating away from public view. Bulimics may pick up several cakes at the bakery on the way home from work, explaining to the clerk that they are having a party. By the time they get home, the binge may be complete—all the cake is gone and they are ready to purge. Or bulimics may purposely stay awake after everyone else has gone to sleep so that they can finish several quarts of ice cream in the freezer undetected, replacing them in the morning before anyone in the house notices their absence.

For the most part, the binging is done quickly. In fact, bulimics will often gulp and swallow the food without even tasting it. After the first few minutes, a binge has no relationship to hunger. It stops only when the food runs out or when the bulimics are interrupted by someone who must be kept in the dark about what is happening. As the binge continues, it often produces a repetitive, antidepressant sensation similar to that produced by swimming or running.

In many cases, a binge episode is triggered when bulimics pass an invisible limit they have set for themselves. This may mean eating one bite over a self-prescribed food limit—perhaps two teaspoons of ice cream instead of one. Although the number varies in each individual case, bulimics will usually binge and purge at least once a day, with the average being 12 times a week. (The frequency can range from once a week to 46 times a week.)

In one study, conducted by Dr. James Edward Mitchell at the

University of Minnesota, half of the bulimic respondents reported that they consumed more than 3,400 calories in a typical binge. By contrast, the normal daily intake for a moderately active female is 2,500 calories and for a moderately active male 3,000 calories. The binges usually lasted less than two hours, but they could last as long as eight hours.

The foods most commonly eaten during a binge are ice cream, bread, candy, doughnuts, soft drinks, sandwiches, cookies, popcorn, milk, cheese, and cereal. According to the Center for the Study of Anorexia and Bulimia (CSAB), although bingers are partial to junk food, many bulimics binge on the food that they feel they have recently eaten too much of. In these cases bulimics feel that they are punishing themselves by binging on that food.

The frequency of the purging and binging, however, is not really the essential part of the disease. What is most important to discover, and what vary in each and every case, are the emotions that are being masked by the bulimic behavior. Dr. Rabinor illustrates this with an example from a therapy group she runs for bulimic women. All of these women, she points out, are extremely attractive, yet they all spend a tremendous amount of

According to the Center for the Study of Anorexia and Bulimia, many bulimics binge on junk food because it is readily available and easily consumed.

time each day thinking about food, shopping for food, planning meals, and worrying about their body. One woman related an incident that occurred at 2:00 A.M. Her baby began to cry, and as she walked to his room to quiet him down, all she could think about was her thighs. She thought about how fat they were, how they rubbed against one another, and how disgusted with herself they made her feel. To the group this did not seem unusual; many of the other bulimics thought the same thing about themselves, whether it was two in the morning or two in the afternoon.

With some direction from Rabinor, the new mother, as well as the other members of her group, came to see that thinking about her thighs allowed this young woman not to face her feeling of anger at that moment. Why was she angry? There were a number of reasons: She was angry with the baby for waking her up; she was angry with her husband for sleeping through the crying; she was angry with her situation because she missed the excitement and freedom of her life before the baby was born. It was too difficult, however, for her to face these feelings—this anger—a difficulty made worse for the bulimic because she has often spent most of her life not facing problems. So instead of exploring her feelings, the woman focused on the self-hatred she felt for being "fat" and having tremendous thighs—a feeling triggered, perhaps, because she ate one extra cookie during the day.

In addition to their eating problems, or in some cases because of them, bulimics are often socially isolated. They know they have a problem and often think they are the only people in the world with their problem. Their eating behavior takes up so much of their time and thoughts that there may be nothing left over for other people. Also, according to Drs. James Mitchell and Richard L. Phyle and Elke D. Eckert, M.C., bulimics, who are already abusing food, are at a higher risk to abuse other substances, including drugs and alcohol.

Much like anorexics, bulimics have physical symptoms that are physiological manifestations of their disease. If the person is using vomiting as a method of purging, these symptoms and effects can include:

1. Difficulty swallowing and retaining food.

2. Swollen and/or infected salivary glands.

A 1901 advertisement for laxatives. People who abuse laxatives can suffer stomach and other muscle cramps and digestive problems.

3. Damage to the esophagus, sometimes causing pain and/or internal bleeding.

4. Burst blood vessels in the eyes.

5. Excessive tooth decay and loss of tooth enamel.

People who abuse laxatives can suffer from

1. Muscle cramps.

2. Stomach cramps.

3. Digestive problems.

4. Dizziness.

5. Colon failure.

6. Heart failure.

Other symptoms, which may result from either the binging or the purging, include weakness, headaches, dizziness, nausea, and diabetes. Especially when binges consist primarily of sweets, symptoms may include electrolyte imbalances—that is, disruption of the essential chemical balance of the body's fluids—and potassium depletion.

PROFILE OF A BULIMIC: JOANNE'S STORY

During the time when I suffered from bulimia, I would feel full from tiny amounts. If I ever went beyond the full feeling by even one bite, I knew I would be throwing up later, so I would eat whatever was around. It could be three yogurts, two or three eggs in an omelet, a box of cookies, two English muffins. This eating was not enjoyable, but to me it was necessary. It was done quickly, hand to mouth, without pausing to taste the food or to think what was happening. It was true binging, obsessive behavior. I would feel terrible and guilty that I had eaten so much, and I worried that I might get fat. Then I would throw up. As a dancer I had such good muscles that I did not even have to tickle my throat. I would just contract my stomach and it would all come up. At the height of the disease I would do this two or three times a day. The eating was oppressive, but the throwing up was "liberating."

Compulsive Overeating

Compulsive overeating is a separate eating disorder, but it is really very similar to bulimia. The only difference is that compulsive overeaters do not purge. Often, they too eat to combat stress, binging on large amounts of food. Though they do not suffer from many of the symptoms and side effects that occur as a result of the purging aspect of bulimia, compulsive overeaters often have medical problems nonetheless. Many are overweight—some to the point of obesity (being 20% to 30% overweight). This, in turn, weakens the heart and can lead to death. Compulsive overeating over the long term can also lead to high blood pressure, diabetes, and heart disease—all diseases associated with being overweight. In addition, because they may often binge on junk food or one particular food, compulsive overeaters can suffer from nutritional shortcomings as well.

PROFILE OF A COMPULSIVE OVEREATER: CAROLE'S STORY

The urge to binge would come as I was driving home from work. I would start feeling miserable thinking about what I had to do and who I might have offended and wondering if I would be fired, and the first thing I wanted to do was stuff food in my mouth. Before I got home I would stop at a Pepperidge Farm store and buy a cake and eat it as I drove, holding it in my hand. Sometimes the cake was partially frozen, and by the time I got home the car and I were a mess. But by that time I had stuffed my feelings. The pain that I could not handle was gone.

I would often binge on an evening or a weekend when I had nothing to do, so that I would not feel lonely. I ate to relieve stress, boredom, anxiety. . . . I never ate when I was happy. I ate to fill time. After a while, the eating would make me fall asleep, which would take up some of the empty time and prevent me from having to do anything else.

Sometimes, after eating the cake, I would eat dinner, and then I would eat everything that was in the house. It did not matter what it was. If I had bread and butter I would have one slice and eat it in the living room. Then I would go in and get another, then a third, then I would make a sandwich and the whole loaf of bread would soon be gone. At the end of the binge, if I was still awake I felt that the food was not doing its job, so I would keep eating until it did.

I used to go the supermarket on the weekend and buy every carbohydrate that anyone could imagine having at a birthday party. I would buy ice cream and cakes, cookies and pretzels, and then I would have my own birthday party all weekend in my house. My weeks were so filled with pressure that this was a way to forget about them for two days.

I tried every food in the supermarket—meats, potato chips, sweets, pasta dishes. I would give in to every urge that I had. I kept looking for the one thing that would make me feel better.

The feeling that would come before a binge was that I had no control over that behavior, that the urge to keep eating had overwhelmed me. I would think, "I am going to walk into that store and buy that cake," or "I am going to walk into that restaurant even though I feel fat and disgusting and the place itself is disgusting. There is no way I can stop myself." And then I wanted the food so much I could not stop myself even if I really wanted to.

When I was eating the food I had no control either. I could not stop until I fell asleep or got physically sick, or, sometimes, threw up . . . and then I would eat more. When I was little my younger sister and I used to sneak food together, stopping only when our mother found us. I learned early on, though, to flush food down the toilet and to hide cupcake wrappers in the medicine chest.

Before I joined Overeaters Anonymous, I craved food every 10 minutes. Food was a drug that had stopped working for me. It no longer made me feel better. I would eat so much at night that I could not get up to be at work on time, and I desperately needed my job.

Today, Carole is in her mid-forties. She is divorced, holds an important job, and is the mother of a teenage girl.

In the next chapter the psychological traits characteristic of an eating-disorder sufferer will be discussed and the factors causing such disorders explored.

·　　　·　　　·　　　·

CHAPTER 6

WHO ARE THE VICTIMS?

Although it is impossible to predict exactly who will develop an eating disorder, studies have shown that the typical anorexic is female (85% to 95%) and fairly young, mostly between 13 and 25 years of age. Anorexia is rare among older women. According to Dr. April Benson, a psychologist associated with the CSAB, older women who stop eating usually do so because they have suffered a significant loss, such as death or divorce; the appetite loss is a depressed reaction to a concrete external

Singer Karen Carpenter, shown here with her brother, Richard (left), and musician Herb Alpert, died in 1983 from complications of anorexia.

cause, as opposed to the more complicated psychological suffering of most younger self-starvers.

Anorexia is also more likely to strike people whose appearance is the focus of their careers—dancers, actors, models, flight attendants, jockeys, gymnasts, and professional runners. Gelsey Kirkland, a former principal dancer with the New York City Ballet and the American Ballet Theatre, describes the obsession in her autobiography (written with Greg Lawrence), *Dancing on My Grave*. "Mr. B.'s ideal proportions called for an almost skeletal frame, accentuating the collarbones and length of the neck. Defeminization was the overall result, with the frequent cessation of the menstrual cycle due to malnutrition and physical abuse. . . . This 'concentration camp' aesthetic leads to self abuse of diet pills, quack weight-reducing formulas, and ultimately, anorexia." (Mr. B. was George Balanchine, the artistic director of the New York City Ballet, whose advice was not "eat less" but "eat nothing.")

Bulimia sufferers are from a broader socioeconomic background and an older age group than anorexics are. One reason for the delayed onset is that bulimia sometimes develops as a response to the extreme starvation of anorexia (early in anorexia, when the sufferer still feels hunger) or to years of somewhat more moderate dieting, which still leave the dieter chronically hungry.

PSYCHOLOGICAL CHARACTERISTICS

It is important to note that not all people suffering from an eating disorder display the same symptoms or act in the same manner. Eating disorders also afflict a wide variety of people from different backgrounds and age groups. The following characteristics, then, are a composite of a typical, or average, sufferer—but they do not describe all sufferers.

Anorexics tend to be teenagers and young women who are well behaved, eager to please, and require no special attention. Their eagerness to please often means that instead of developing independent desires, they try to discover and do exactly what their parents want. All eating-disorder sufferers have a low opinion of themselves and depend to a great extent on the opinions of others to make them feel good about themselves. Because they can never be sure of what those opinions will be, and because they are never independently pleased with themselves, anorexics are total perfectionists. They need to do well in school and sports, to look wonderful, and to be invited to every party. At the same time, they are critical of themselves and often think they are bad people with evil thoughts who do not deserve the presents and attention they receive from their parents.

Anorexics have a difficult time achieving independence, which is one of the major reasons that the disease appears at just those times in life when independence is expected. However, the problems really begin to take root much earlier.

Bulimia

A composite personality of a bulimic is more difficult to devise. In fact, there are many personality types who become bulimic, ranging from those who are attractive, successful perfectionists to those who are sloppy, lead chaotic lives, and may suffer from other disorders such as depression, psychosis, or substance abuse. For the latter group, as with most eating-disorder sufferers, bulimia is just one of several symptoms of their problems.

Bulimics share many of the psychological characteristics and family situations that Hilde Bruch and others attributed originally to anorexics. Bulimics, however, are often more skillful than anorexics at hiding both the causes and the symptoms of their disease behind a facade of independence and achievement. This may be because bulimics are usually older than anorexics and also because bulimics are often of normal weight or are only slightly overweight, so their behavior as well as their problems are not obvious to the untrained observer. In fact, one of the difficulties therapists have in treating bulimics is that sufferers mask their psychological problems so effectively that they think that their eating behavior is their only problem. This makes these bulimics extremely resistant to the type of therapy that may be required before they can live healthy lives.

Many bulimics are obsessed with body size and with excelling at sports.

What follows is a list of some of the characteristics that may predispose a person to become a bulimic or a compulsive over-eater (compulsive overeating is a disease that shares many of the same symptoms as bulimia):

1. Low self-esteem—constantly trying to please and win the praise of others, because bulimics cannot give praise to themselves.

2. Perfectionism, especially with regard to looks and achievement. Gretchen Goff, a former bulimic who has written a pamphlet on the subject, describes the way perfectionism interacts with the disorder: "Bulimics might be somewhat perfectionistic. . . . but as a result of becoming bulimics they become extremely so. Because they see themselves as awful people who binge/vomit, their expectations of themselves become more outrageous, and they have to flip into total perfectionism."

3. Obsession with body size and food. Many bulimics have tried dieting for years. They may be convinced that their body size is much too large.

4. Confusion resulting from identity crisis. Bulimics may not be able to effectively develop a sense of identity through the normal means, such as friendships, achievements, etc.

5. Immature and black-and-white thinking.

6. Suppression of feelings, especially anger. The bulimic often conceals strong emotions; anger or stress often leads the bulimic to begin binging rather than confronting his or her problems directly. As this pattern continues, eating becomes such an effective replacement for feeling certain emotions that these feelings do not even surface before the bulimic begins binging. The binging/vomiting aggravates this feeling of distance at the same time that it further numbs the real emotions.

7. Reliance on schedules, lack of spontaneity. Bulimics cannot stand blocks of unplanned time.

8. Sexual problems. These are aggravated because bulimics are so ashamed of their bulimic behavior that they cannot risk the exposure that true intimacy requires—many, too, are not comfortable with their sexuality and may refrain from becoming sexually involved in any way.

9. Lack of autonomy. Bulimics, despite appearances to the contrary, are dependent on those around them and devastated by rejection.

10. Clinical depression. Bulimics are often ~~depressed~~. There is debate, however, as to whether depression is a cause or a result of the disorder.

Compulsive Overating

Although compulsive overeaters share many of the traits of bulimics and anorexics, there is often a difference in why they eat. In *Fat Is a Family Affair*, Dr. Judi Hollis writes, addressing the sufferer: "Your decision to develop an eating disorder actually had some wisdom. It saved you from the painful realizations and disappointments that accompany the difference between you and other people—the reality that they may not be there for you. Since you felt you could not weather those disappointments, you decided to nurture yourself without them. That's what binging does. You are totally safe and secure while binging."

EATING DISORDERS AND THE BODY

Research cited by Dr. Walter Kaye, a University of Pittsburgh psychiatrist, may help to explain why an anorexic may get some pleasure from his or her weight loss and may thus be so unwilling to end it. Dr. Kaye's research dealt with endorphins, neurotransmitters in the brain that heighten the sense of pleasure and dull the reception of pain. Because of their similarity to opiates (opiates are psychoactive drugs derived from the opium plant), endorphins are often known as the body's natural opiates. The starvation and frenetic physical activity of the anorexic cause the level of endorphins in the brain to increase to twice the level present in the same patient after he or she has gained weight. These physiological changes, Dr. Kaye stresses, allow a person to continue dieting long after the pain of hunger has forced other people to stop. This prolongation of dieting gives anorexia its special character. In other words, these dieters can continue because their starvation has produced a euphoria similar to that produced by mind-altering drugs or exercise, as in the "runner's high."

Dr. Judith Wurtman, a scientist at the Massachusetts Institute of Technology, has studied why people crave carbohydrates, and she says that eating carbohydrates stimulates the production of serotonin, a neurotransmitter in the brain. When this occurs, people feel calmer and better able to cope. For this reason, bulimics, as well as those who do not suffer from eating disorders, will crave carbohydrates such as sugar and starch when under stress.

Eating-Disorder Sufferers and Their Families

The traditional view of the typical eating-disorder sufferer's family was developed by Dr. Bruch from observations of her anorexic patients. Her belief was that such families lavish material goods, educational and recreational opportunities, and emotional attention on their daughters. Superficially, the families run smoothly. Underneath the smiles, however, there is tension and confusion—problems that the family denies rather than confronting.

These are families whose members cannot communicate well with each other. As Dr. Rabinor pointed out in a 1988 interview, "Where communication is good and family members turn to each other when there are problems, they do not turn to the refrigerator."

In therapy, said Bruch, these families can always interpret the feelings of others, but they cannot openly express their own feelings. They are excessively concerned about how things will look to the outside world and often say, "This is not done," about some behavior of which they disapprove.

The relationship between mother and daughter is probably most crucial to this psychological interpretation of conditions that could lead to an eating disorder. The mothers of anorexics may be excessively intrusive, leaving their daughters little privacy. In fact, says Dr. Benson, anorexia may be seen as pushing food away to keep out an intrusive mother, whereas bulimia is more likely to develop in a person who has been desperate for attention.

Another way in which an anorexic's relationship with her mother may be abnormal involves the relationship between the mother and father. Such cases often involve role reversal; that is, the daughter often feels that she must nurture her mother to make up for what she knows to be her mother's less-than-satisfying relationship with her father. Because the mother has turned to the daughter with *her* problems, the daughter feels that there is nowhere for her to turn when *she* is troubled. This feeling of having no place to go for help is one reason many people with eating disorders wait so long before seeking treatment.

Therapists have also discovered that there are other family situations that can predispose a person to an eating disorder. These include families that are chaotic and likely to contain at least one member who is a substance (alcohol, drug, or food) abuser. This view goes hand in hand with evidence that a higher-than-average percentage of people with eating disorders have been the victims of rape, incest, molestation, verbal abuse, and neglect. These people then turn excessively to or away from food because they have no other way to express their fear, anger, and confusion.

In the next chapter, different treatment programs—designed to meet the needs of particular eating-disorder sufferers—will be discussed.

•   •   •   •

CHAPTER 7

GETTING HELP

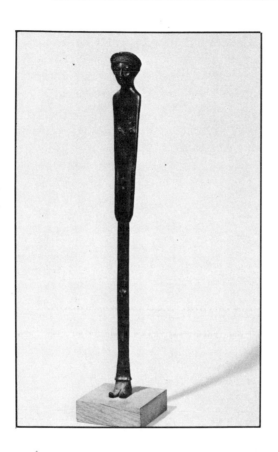

People suffering from eating disorders cannot help themselves. Although they may be able to stop for a short time,
in the long run they will be back on the path of self-destruction.
If left untreated, eating disorders may eventually lead to death.
Treatment, however, does not simply involve forcing an anorexic
to eat or teaching a bulimic or compulsive overeater the basics
of a good diet. Rather, the underlying emotional causes—the
disturbances that lie at the root of the disorder—must also be

uncovered and resolved in order for treatment to be successful.

In light of this necessity, the most effective treatment for an eating-disorder sufferer combines medical attention to cure the patient's physical ailments with psychotherapy to help the patient understand the cause of the behavior. It is also important that treatment begin as soon as there is a suspicion that an eating disorder may be present. Early treatment is essential because it gives doctors a better chance of arresting and reversing the physical and psychological symptoms and side effects that accompany eating disorders. If left unchecked, the damage—both physiological and psychological—may be irreversible.

In fact, according to Dr. Bruch, if starvation is allowed to persist it can cause personality distortions, which can lead a patient to the edge of schizophrenia. Because of the dangers that prolonged eating disorders can pose, parents or other relatives

Early detection and treatment provides a better chance of arresting the destructive behavior that can result from eating disorders.

and friends must insist that the sufferer get treatment, regardless of what he or she says.

When logic does not work, rewards and punishments must be used. If the eating-disorder sufferer is living at home, the most effective method of getting him or her into psychological treatment, as well as a good way to see that treatment is effective, is for the family to enter therapy together.

CHOOSING A COURSE OF THERAPY

There are a number of different medical and psychological methods used to treat eating-disorder sufferers. A person should choose a program that suits his or her needs and, preferably, one that has been successful with a number of patients. Not every program suits every patient's needs, and this, perhaps, is a reflection of the uniqueness of each case. Dr. Craig Johnson, an expert in the causes and treatment of anorexia and bulimia, points out in Jane Cawel's book *Bulimia,* "To say that a certain treatment will work for everybody ignores the uniqueness of human behavior. Effective treatment requires a very complete, accurate assessment of the physiological, psychological, and cultural dimensions of the individual."

An assessment should be done by a center for eating disorders, a reputable organization dedicated to helping sufferers, or a specialist recommended by a trusted physician. (In addition, there is a list of organizations that can be of further help in the back of this volume.) Treatment may vary in length as well as method. It may range from a few months to several years and from once-a-week treatment as an outpatient to hospitalization for those whose starvation has proceeded to the point where their life is at risk.

Medical Treatment for Eating Disorders

Anorexics who have lost 30% or more of their body weight may be in immediate danger of losing their life and often require hospitalization to help them gain some weight. Unfortunately, most anorexics strongly resist this step. Until they have benefited from some treatment, most anorexics still see themselves as fat and are terrified at the prospect of being forced to gain weight.

Even in the hospital they often use clever maneuvers to dispose of food without eating it. Hospital personnel, however, are becoming more and more aware of this behavior. Some hospitals, for instance, remove all garbage cans and plants so that anorexics cannot easily dispose of or bury their food.

It is crucial, however, that an anorexic gain weight in order to make a complete recovery. This is not only to alleviate physical symptoms but also, as Dr. Bruch pointed out, to alleviate psychological symptoms because there can be no effective psychotherapy when the patient is suffering from the distorted thoughts brought on by starvation, including an obsessive focus on food.

In many cases, however, the anorexic refuses to eat. If this occurs, there are a number of ways in which the physician can get the patient to take in nourishment. The first is to feed the patient through a tube inserted in the stomach. This method, however, is painful and is also considered a way of punishing the patient for his or her refusal to eat. A much more popular method is the insertion of an intravenous (into the vein) tube through which nutrients flow directly into the blood.

The most commonly used method to induce a change in eating behavior—one that is helpful with bulimics as well as anorexics—is behavior modification. This method proceeds from the theory that abnormal behavior has been learned and is somehow being reinforced (rewarded). Thus, the goal is to teach and reinforce new behavior. For instance, if the patient must gain weight, he or she may be required to remain in bed or in one room on any day that he or she refuses to eat. When the scale shows an increase, the patient might be rewarded with phone, visiting, or grounds-walking privileges. However, a clever patient can figure out how to make the scale move temporarily without really changing his or her true weight (by drinking water beforehand, or adding extra clothing or weights), and the manipulative ability of anorexic patients often makes them extremely difficult to treat. In the long run, however, such disruptive tactics are not successful, as the staff of the treatment center or hospital becomes aware of the patient's tricks, or the physician orders more drastic measures be taken (such as forced tube feeding).

For bulimics, behavior modification (which for bulimics is unlikely to take place in a hospital setting) might include interruption of the binge/purge cycle, self-monitoring via a daily diary, the introduction of regular eating habits (for the first time in some patients), limiting the amount of food per meal, limiting foods high in carbohydrates in the home, and avoiding high-risk situations, such as unstructured time.

Therapists differ as to how they view behavior modification. Dr. Bruch feels that it can be harmful because "its very efficiency increases the inner turmoil and sense of helplessness in these youngsters who feel tricked into relinquishing the last vestige of control over their bodies and their lives." She further cautions that weight gain without psychotherapy can make patients more miserable than they were before treatment.

On the other hand, Dr. Benson views behavior modification as "essential" once a sufferer has reached the stage of needing hospitalization. "These girls have never had firm limits before," she stresses, "and the rewards and consequences of a behavior modification program make them feel more like other people, not quite so precious. Now there are concrete limits against which they may, finally, be able to express anger."

Scientists and physicians seem to differ on the subject of behavior modification depending upon whether they see it as a useful addition to psychotherapy, a foundation for psychotherapy, or the solution to the problem. Geneen Roth, a researcher who works with compulsive overeaters, is strongly against using behavior modification as the only treatment and instructs the patients she works with to begin to help themselves by not dieting and instead eating whatever they want. She points out in her book *Feeding the Hungry Heart:*

> When you believe your hunger is related to something as controllable as the shape of your body, you don't have to undergo the sometimes lengthy and often painful questioning of other things about yourself. You don't have to come face-to-face with empty dreams or the lack of fulfillment you experience in your work and/or relationships. You can decide that your troubles are weight-related—and then continue to eat compulsively.

If the patient is not in a life-threatening situation and the decision is made to use both behavior modification and psychotherapy, there is a question as to which should come first. Some bulimics may have to change their behavior before they can feel good enough about themselves to benefit from therapy, whereas others may require therapy to change their behavior. As one woman said, "Bulimia hid all my feelings, and when I uncovered them, the binges stopped working."

Regardless of the timing of the therapy, or whether or not it is used in conjunction with behavior modification, psychotherapy is used, at some point, in the majority of cases. The next chapter will explore psychotherapy, its use in treating patients with eating disorders, and how to choose a competent therapist.

•　　　•　　　•　　　•

CHAPTER 8

PSYCHOTHERAPY AND OA

The typical sufferer of an eating disorder will resist any kind of treatment. This resistance is not limited to such methods as forced feeding, which is designed to directly add weight to the patient, but also includes psychotherapy. Many anorexics fear that therapy will rob them of their special diet, which they feel is essential to their sense of control. In addition, many patients in the later stages of the disease often deny or do not recognize that they have a problem—obviously, such denial also hinders psychotherapy.

Bulimics and compulsive overeaters, on the other hand, recognize that they have a problem but often believe that the issue is strictly limited to their eating behavior and is not a reflection of an emotional maladjustment requiring psychotherapy. These people believe, as Geneen Roth writes in *Feeding the Hungry Heart*, that one last diet will make them well. However, once a woman has gone from being anorexic to being bulimic, she may be more likely to seek treatment as she comes to see that, although her behavior may be changing, she is still obsessed with food.

Dr. Bruch warned that traditional Freudian psychiatric treatment, focusing on interpreting the patient's thoughts and dreams, may not be appropriate for a young person with an eating disorder. This form of treatment may in fact be a reminder of the situation that brought on the disorder. For these people, hearing someone else tell them what their feelings mean can make them feel as though their feelings are not their own and that they do not understand their own thoughts.

Instead, the CSAB recommends that treatment be active, encouraging the patient to think for him- or herself and supporting his or her efforts to become independent. For psychotherapy to be successful, therefore, the patient must find a therapist who can be trusted. There are many different personalities and approaches in therapy, and no one therapist, no matter what his or her reputation, will do well with every patient. Successful therapy requires the patient and therapist to interact continually, so that at the very least there must be the same kind of rapport between them that is found in a good friendship. If the whole family is to go together, which many organizations recommend, all members must be able to work with the therapist. The family members must feel able to tell all their secrets, dreams, fears, and fantasies to the therapist without fear of being judged in any way. This skill of objective observation, in addition to intuitively knowing what questions to ask so that the patient begins to develop some insights into his or her behavior, are just two of the characteristics of a good psychotherapist.

Most bulimics who enter psychotherapy are also required by their therapists to enter group therapy, at the same time or at a later point. In this group situation, people with similar problems talk to each other under the direction of a therapist in an attempt to further understand how they relate to other people. For bulimics, group therapy is particularly important. Many view their behavior, and thus themselves, as disgusting and have gradually stopped all social contact except that contact absolutely required for work or school. Often other group members are the first people (aside from a therapist) to know about their eating disorder. With others who are similarly afflicted, many bulimics can relax and be themselves. Revealing who and what they are comes as an enormous relief. By making friends and growing to like and accept other bulimics, the bulimic works toward the difficult goal of liking and accepting him- or herself.

Overeaters Anonymous

Another approach to treating eating disorders does not fit exactly into the mold of psychotherapy or behavior modification. Overeaters Anonymous (OA) is a group that has programs for anorexics and bulimics as well as for compulsive overeaters. The basis of OA is a program based on the concepts that have made Alcoholics Anonymous (a similar program, started in the 1930s, whose aim is to help alcoholics deal with their problem and refrain from drinking) so successful.

People in OA say that their food addiction is a disease they will have for life; therefore, they are always recovering. Part of OA's philosophy is that addicts should learn to turn to people rather than to food. The many OA meetings that are held all over the country at all times of the night and day help make this turning to people possible.

OA differs from psychotherapy in several important ways. In the first place, psychotherapy sessions cost money, whereas OA meetings are free. In the second, OA focuses more on group interaction and less on the individual. Finally, where psychotherapy stresses giving patients the skills to gain control over their life, OA stresses spirituality and asks participants to relinquish control to a "higher power."

OA has eight tools. These are

1. Abstaining from compulsive eating. For members of OA, compulsive eating is a symptom of their addiction to food. This symptom must be dealt with on a daily basis.

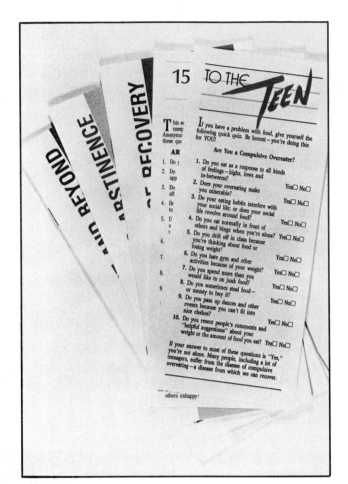

Publications distributed by Overeaters Anonymous. This literature is one of the eight tools each OA member uses in his or her fight against food addiction.

2. Sponsoring an OA member. Sponsors are OA members who are following the traditions and steps, abstaining from compulsive overeating, and are willing to share their experiences with a newer member.

3. Attending meetings. The actual number is up to the individual. A participant might attend one meeting a week, three to five a week, or more than one a day. Meetings may be large groups of people coming together, or simply two members discussing their problems with compulsive overeating.

4. Making phone calls. Each OA participant is encouraged to make phone calls to other members or their sponsor. This is to help food addicts, who are often isolated, to turn to people instead of to food.

5. Writing out feelings, problems, and inventories. Members are encouraged to write out "inventories" of people they have hurt and to put on paper their everyday feelings and problems. In this way, members will be more in touch with the ways they really feel and less likely to eat compulsively.

6. Studying and reading OA literature. Members are encouraged to read the books and pamphlets published by OA. Daily reading of this literature can help to reaffirm the steps and traditions.

7. Maintaining anonymity. At meetings members identify themselves only by first name. This allows them to open up in a safe environment, and to put "principles before their personalities."

8. Performing some service to OA. This can mean becoming a sponsor, taking someone to a meeting, or setting up the chairs for a meeting. The idea is that if one gives something, one gets back more in return.

Many recovered eating-disorder sufferers are able, for the first time in their life, to feel good about themselves and not use food to mask their true feelings.

Once the behavioral symptoms of eating disorders have been stopped or reduced, regardless of the type of therapy chosen, the psychological goals are for the sufferer to become independent and more confident. It is important for patients undergoing therapy to keep in mind that a cure is possible, even though it may take a long time and a lot of hard work. Recovery occurs when the patient can identify the causes of his or her abnormal eating behavior and find a better way of dealing with them than binging on food. Many recovering bulimics, anorexics, and compulsive overeaters are able, often for the first time in their life, to feel good about themselves, to form relationships, to hold down jobs or to attend school, to discuss and express their feelings, and to act assertively to get what they want out of life.

•　　　　•　　　　•　　　　•

APPENDIX 1:
FOOD GROUPS

To help people choose foods that put the right kind of variety into their diet, the American Dietetic Association recommends eating foods every day from each of five basic food groups, in the following amounts:

Basic Group	Examples	Amounts
Breads, cereals, and other grain products	Whole wheat bread, corn flakes	6–11 servings a day, including several whole-grain products
Fruit	Oranges, apples, bananas, melon, berries	2–4 servings a day
Vegetables	Spinach, sweet and white potatoes, carrots, broccoli, peas	3–5 servings, include all types regularly and dark green leafy vegetables and dried beans and peas several times a week
Meat, poultry, fish, and alternates all of which provide protein	Hamburger, chicken, turkey, flounder, shrimp, eggs, peanut butter	2–3 servings, totaling 5–7 ounces of lean protein
Dairy products	Milk, cheese, yogurt	2–3/men, 3–4/women, 2 or more for children, 4 or more for teens and women who are pregnant or are breast-feeding

APPENDIX 2:
FOR MORE INFORMATION

The following is a list of organizations and associations that can provide further information on eating disorders.

American Anorexia/Bulimia
   Association (AABA)
133 Cedar Lane
Teaneck, NJ 07666
(201) 863-1800

American Dietetic Association
430 North Michigan Avenue
Chicago, IL 60611

Anorexia and Bulimia Resource
   Center
2699 South Bayshore
Suite 800 E
Coconut Grove, FL 33133
(305) 854-0652

Anorexia and Bulimia Treatment
   and Education Center
(800) 33-ABTEC
(301) 332-9800 in MD

Anorexia Nervosa and Related
   Eating Disorders, Inc.
   (ANRED)
P.O. Box 5102
Eugene, OR 97405
(503) 344-1144

Breaking Free Seminars
   (Compulsive Overeating)
Expo Associates
452 Eston Road
Wellesley, MA 02181
(617) 431-7807

Center for the Study of Anorexia
   and Bulimia (CSAB)
1 West 91st Street
New York, NY 10024
(212) 595-3449

Eating Disorders Center
330 West 58th Street
Suite 200
New York, NY 10019
(212) 582-1345

Food and Drug Administration
Office of Consumer Affairs
5600 Fishers Lane
HFE-88
Rockville, MD 20857
(301) 443-3170

Food and Nutrition Information
   Center
National Agricultural Library
Room 304
Beltsville, MD 20705
(301) 344-3719

National Anorexia Aid Society
The Bridge Foundation
5796 Karl Road
Columbus, OH 43229
(614) 436-1112
(614) 846-2833

National Cholesterol Education
   Program Information Center
4733 Bethesda Avenue, Room 530
Bethesda, MD 20814
(301) 951-3260

UTAH

University of Utah School of
 Medicine
Eating Disorders Clinic
50 North Medical Drive
Salt Lake City, UT 84132
(801) 581-8989

VIRGINIA

Medical College of Virginia
Eating Disorders Program
MCV Station, Box 710
Richmond, VA 23298
(804) 786-9157
(804) 786-0762

WISCONSIN

University of Wisconsin Hospital
 and Clinics
Eating Disorders Program
Madison, WI 53706
(608) 263-6406

Hot Lines

Glenbeigh Food Addictions Hot Line
(800) 4A-BINGE

ODZPNP National Health Infor-
mation Center
(800) 336-4797
(301) 565-4167

FURTHER READING

Bennett, William, M.D., and Joel Gurin. *The Dieter's Dilemma.* New York: Basic Books, 1983.

Berland, Theodore. *Rating the Diets.* New York: Signet, 1986.

Brody, Jane. *Jane Brody's Nutrition Book.* New York: Bantam, 1981.

Bruch, Hilde. *The Golden Cage.* New York: Random House, 1978.

Brumberg, Joan Jacobs. *Fasting Girls: The Emergence of Anorexia Nervosa as a Modern Disease.* Cambridge: Harvard University Press, 1988.

Cauwels, Janice. *Bulimia: The Binge-Purge Compulsion.* Garden City, NY: Doubleday, 1983.

Chernin, Kim. *The Obsession: Reflections of the Tyranny of Slenderness.* New York: Harper & Row, 1982.

Erlanger, Ellen. *Eating Disorders: A Question and Answer Book About Anorexia Nervosa and Bulimia Nervosa.* Minneapolis: Lerner, 1988.

Garner, David, and Paul E. Garfinkel. "Cultural Expectation of Thinness in Women." *Psychological Reports* 47 (1980): 483–91.

———. *Handbook of Psychotherapy for Anorexia Nervosa and Bulimia.* New York: Guilford, 1985.

———. "An Overview of the Socio-cultural Factors in the Development of Anorexia Nervosa." *In Anorexia Nervosa: Recent Developments.* New York: Alan R. Liss, 1983.

———. *The Role of Drug Treatments for Eating Disorders.* New York: Brunner-Mazel, 1987.

Herzog, David, M.D., Martin B. Keller, M.D., and Phillip Lavori. "Outcome of Anorexia Nervosa and Bulimia Nervosa." *The Journal of Nervous and Mental Disease*, March 1988.

Hirschmann, Jane, and Carol Munter. *Overcoming Overeating*. Indianapolis: Addison-Wesley, 1988.

Hollis, Judi. *Fat Is a Family Affair*. Center City, MN: Hazelden, 1985.

Hornyak, Lynn M., and Ellen K. Baker, eds. *Experimental Therapies for Eating Disorders*. New York: Guilford, 1989.

Jacobson, Michael F. *The Complete Eater's Digest and Nutrition Scoreboard: The Consumer's Factbook of Food Additives and Healthful Eating*. Garden City, NY: Anchor Press/Doubleday, 1985.

Kennedy, Sidney, and Paul E. Garfinkel. "Anorexia Nervosa." *American Psychiatric Association's Annual Review* 4 (1985).

Kolodny, Nancy J. *When Food's a Foe: How to Confront and Conquer Eating Disorders*. Boston: Little, Brown, 1987.

Larocca, Felix E. F., ed. *The Psychiatric Clinics of North America, Symposium on Eating Disorders*. Philadelphia: Saunders, 1984.

Levenkron, Steven. *The Best Little Girl in the World*. Chicago: Contemporary Books, 1978.

Orbach, Susie. *Fat Is a Feminist Issue: A Self-Help Guide for Compulsive Eaters*. New York: Berkley, 1978.

Palmer, R. L. *Anorexia Nervosa: A Guide for Sufferers and Their Families*. London: Penguin, 1980.

Pope, Harrison G., Jr., M.D., and James I. Hudson, M.D., "Is Bulimia Nervosa a Heterogeneous Disorder?" *International Journal of Eating Disorders* (February 1988).

Roth, Geneen. *Breaking Free from Compulsive Overeating*. New York: Signet, 1986.

———. *Feeding the Hungry Heart: The Experiences of Compulsive Eating*. New York: New American Library, 1982.

Schachter, S. "Obesity and Overeating." *Science* 161 (1968): 751.

Siegel, Michele, Judith Brisman, and Margot Weinshel. *Surviving an Eating Disorder*. New York: Harper & Row, 1988.

Simms, Ethan Allen Hitchcock. "Experimental Obesity in Men." *Transcript of the Association of American Physicians* 81 (1968): 153.

Wardell, Judy. *Thin Within*. New York: Harmony, 1986.

Wise, Jonathan Kurland, and Susan Kierr Wise. *The Overeaters*. New York: Human Sciences Press, 1979.

GLOSSARY

adipose tissue fatty connective tissue found under the skin and surrounding various body organs

alimentary canal the digestive tube extending from the mouth to the
anus; includes the mouth, pharynx, esophagus, stomach, and small
and large intestines

anorexia nervosa a mental illness characterized by the fear of eating
or gaining weight

appetite suppressant a drug that inhibits the desire for food

binge a period of uncontrolled self-indulgence

bulimia an eating disorder characterized by frequent binging and then
purging of food

calorie common term for kilocalorie, a unit of heat needed to raise 1
gram of water 1 degree centigrade at 1 degree of atmospheric pressure; 3,600 calories of food intake translate into 1 pound of weight

carbohydrate a compound, such as sugar or starch, that has a general
biochemical structure composed of carbon, hydrogen, and oxygen;
to be metabolized, all carbohydrates are broken down into glucose;
excess is stored as glycogen or as fat

carotene a yellow pigment found in various plant and animal tissues;
the precursor of vitamin A

cholesterol a fatlike substance found in blood and tissue

colon the main part of the large intestine

compulsive overeating an eating disorder characterized by binging on
food

dehydration a condition resulting from excessive loss of body fluid

diabetes a disease characterized by the body's inability to handle glucose; occurs when the pancreas fails to manufacture insulin, an
essential hormone

digestive system all the organs and glands associated with ingestion and digestion of food

diuretic a substance, especially a drug, that helps the body excrete urine

electrocardiograph (EKG) an instrument for recording the changes of electrical potential occurring during the heartbeat, used especially in diagnosing abnormalities of heart function

electrolyte any substance that, in solution, is capable of conducting electricity by means of its atoms or groups of atoms and in the process is broken down into positively and negatively charged particles

emaciated excessively thin

endorphins neurotransmitters in the brain that heighten the sense of pleasure and dull the reception of pain

esophagus the muscular tube that carries food from the throat to the stomach

euphoria sense of well-being or elation

fat a substance containing one or more fatty acids; the main substance into which excess carbohydrates are converted for storage by the human body

fiber components of food that are resistant to digestion; these substances add bulk to the diet

hallucination mistaken sense impression

hyperactivity excessive muscular activity

hypothalamus the part of the brain that exerts control over the activity of the abdominal organs, water balance, and body temperature

intravenous within or into a vein

ketone a substance that is the end product of fat metabolism

laxative substance taken to help empty the bowels

metabolism the process by which substances within a living organism are chemically broken down in order to release useful energy

mineral a solid, crystalline chemical substance such as iron, potassium, or sodium, produced by inorganic natural processes; some are necessary to maintain health; often ingested in the form of salts

neurasthenia nervous exhaustion, commonly following a depressed state, characterized by weakness or fatigue

nutrient food or any substance that supplies the body with elements necessary for metabolism

obesity a bodily condition in which there is an excess of fat in relation to other body components; presumed to exist when a person is 20% to 30% or more over his or her normal weight

polyunsaturated fat fat in which the carbon atoms contain the lowest amount of hydrogen atoms and thus do not cause a cholesterol problem; found in vegetable oils and fish

prostate small gland situated at the base of the bladder in the male; concerned with the production of semen

psychosomatic illness physical ailment due to emotional causes

psychotherapy a method of treating disease—especially nervous disorders—by psychological means

purge evacuation of food from the body, either by the use of laxatives or by vomiting

saturated fat fat that contains cholesterol; found in meats and animal products

serotonin a naturally occurring compound found in many body tissues—mainly in the gastrointestinal tract—and in lesser amounts in the blood and central nervous system; has a stimulating effect on the circulatory system

starch a granular or powdery complex carbohydrate that is the chief storage form of carbohydrate in plants

starvation being deprived of food—either unwillingly or voluntarily—for a long period of time

sugar a sweet-tasting carbohydrate that dissolves in water

vitamin one of a group of organic substances required (in minute amounts) for healthy growth and development; insufficient amounts of any of the necessary vitamins can result in specific vitamin-deficiency diseases

INDEX

PICTURE CREDITS

Rachel S. Epstein, a free-lance writer, holds an M.B.A. from New York University. Her articles have appeared in the *Wall Street Journal*, the *Washington Post*, *Working Woman*, and *Ms*. She is the author of *Alternative Investments, Careers in the Investment World, Investment Banking*, and *Investments and the Law* for the Chelsea House BASIC INVESTOR'S LIBRARY and of *Careers in Health Care* for the Chelsea House ENCYCLOPEDIA OF HEALTH.

Solomon H. Snyder, M.D., is Distinguished Service Professor of Neuroscience, Pharmacology, and Psychiatry and director of the Department of Neuroscience at the Johns Hopkins University School of Medicine. He has served as president of the Society for Neuroscience and in 1978 received the Albert Lasker Award in Medical Research for his discovery of opiate receptors in the brain. Dr. Snyder is a member of the National Academy of Sciences and a Fellow of the American Academy of Arts and Sciences. He is the author of *Drugs and the Brain, Uses of Marijuana, Madness and the Brain, The Troubled Mind*, and *Biological Aspects of Mental Disorder*. He is also the general editor of Chelsea House's ENCYCLOPEDIA OF PSYCHOACTIVE DRUGS.

C. Everett Koop, M.D., Sc.D., is Surgeon General, Deputy Assistant Secretary for Health, and Director of the Office of International Health of the U. S. Public Health Service. A pediatric surgeon with an international reputation, he was previously surgeon-in-chief of Children's Hospital of Philadelphia and professor of pediatric surgery and pediatrics at the University of Pennsylvania. Dr. Koop is the author of more than 175 articles and books on the practice of medicine. He has served as surgery editor of the *Journal of Clinical Pediatrics* and editor-in-chief of the *Journal of Pediatric Surgery*. Dr. Koop has received nine honorary degrees and numerous other awards, including the Denis Brown Gold Medal of the British Association of Pediatric Surgeons, the William E. Ladd Gold Medal of the American Academy of Pediatrics, and the Copernicus Medal of the Surgical Society of Poland. He is a Chevalier of the French Legion of Honor and a member of the Royal College of Surgeons, London.